T0125957

Wildflowers
of
Florida
Field Guide

by Jaret C. Daniels
and Stan Tekiela

**ADVENTURE PUBLICATIONS
CAMBRIDGE, MINNESOTA**

*To my wife, Stephanie, for her enduring patience
and kind assistance in the field - Jaret*

To my daughter, Abigail Rose, the sweetest flower in my life - Stan

ACKNOWLEDGMENTS

I would like to thank Thomas Emmel, Scott Simpson and Jeffrey Hansen at the Florida Museum of Natural History's McGuire Center for Lepidoptera and Biodiversity for their kind support and assistance. Thanks as well to my parents for encouraging my interest in natural history. Thanks also to Walter S. Judd, University of Florida in Gainesville, for reviewing the book. I would additionally like to acknowledge the Florida Wildflower Foundation for encouraging public awareness of the tremendous diversity of wildflowers found in Florida. - Jaret

Edited by Deborah Walsh

Book and icon design by Jonathan Norberg

Photo credits by photographer and page number:

> **Cover photo: Rose-of-Plymouth** by Jaret C. Daniels
>
> **Tom Barnes/University of Kentucky:** 384 **Ted Bodner/Southern Weed Science Society, Bugwood.org:** 130 **Rick and Nora Bowers:** 276 (both), 378 (fruit) **Shirley Denton:** 218 **Kimra Plaisance:** 222 (fruit) **Stan Tekiela:** 18, 22, 24, 38 (plant), 54 (fruit), 188, 270, 350, 364, 380, 382, 388 (both) **Bob Upcavage:** 298 (flower close-up) **www.southeasternflora.com:** 52 **Jaret C. Daniels:** all other photos

10 9 8 7 6 5 4 3 2

Wildflowers of Florida Field Guide
Copyright © 2010 by Jaret C. Daniels and Stan Tekiela
Published by Adventure Publications, Inc.
310 Garfield Street South
Cambridge, Minnesota 55008
(800) 678-7006
www.adventurepublications.net
Printed in China
ISBN 978-1-59193-252-9 (pbk.)

TABLE OF CONTENTS

FLORIDA AND WILDFLOWERS

Florida is a great place for wildflower enthusiasts! From the slope forests of the panhandle and temperate broadleaf forests in the north, and from the dry prairies and scrub of the central part of the state to the cypress swamps, pine rocklands, and tropical hardwood forests (hammocks) in the south, Florida is fortunate to have an extremely diverse, often unique and a very healthy variety of wonderful wildflowers.

Wildflowers of Florida Field Guide is an easy-to-use field guide to help the curious nature seeker identify 200 of the most common and widespread wildflowers in Florida. It features, with a number of exceptions, the herbaceous wildflowers of Florida. Herbaceous plants have green soft stems and often die back to the ground each autumn. Some plants with woody stems have been included because these particular plants are very common and have large showy flowers.

STRATEGIES FOR IDENTIFYING WILDFLOWERS

Determining the color of the flower is the first step in a simple five-step process to identify a wildflower.

Because this field guide is organized by color, identifying an unknown wildflower is as simple as matching the color of the flower to the color section of the book. The color tabs on each page identify the color section.

The second step in determining the identity of a wildflower is the size. Is it a single flower or a cluster of flowers? Sometimes flowers are made up of many individual flowers in clusters that are perceived to be one larger flower. These are ordered by the size of the cluster, not the individual flower. Therefore, within each color section, the flowers are grouped with the single flowers first, followed by those with flower clusters. Each group is then arranged by size, from small to large. For example, a plant with a single small yellow flower will be in the beginning of the yellow section, while a large white flower cluster will be toward the end of the white section. The size may be shown as a range, with the average used to place the flower in size order. See page 428 for rulers to help estimate flower and leaf sizes.

Once you have determined the color and approximate size, observe the appearance of the flower. For the single flowers, note if the flower has a regular, irregular, bell or tube shape. If it is a cluster, is the general shape of the cluster flat, round or spike? Also, counting the number of petals might help to identify these individual flowers. Compare your findings with the descriptions on each page. Examining the flower as described should reduce identification possibilities of the wildflower to a few candidates.

The fourth step is to look at the leaves. There are several possible shapes or types of leaves. Simple leaves have only one leaf blade, but can be lobed. Compound leaves have a long central leafstalk with many smaller leaflets attached. Twice compound leaves have at least two leafstalks and many leaflets. Sometimes it is helpful to note if the leaves have an edge (margin) that is toothed or smooth, so look for this also. In cacti (one species of which is included in this field guide), the spines are actually modified leaves.

For the fifth step, check how the leaf is attached to the stem. Some plants may look similar, but have different leaf attachments, so this can be very helpful. See if the leaves are attached opposite each other along the stem, alternately, or whorled around a point on the stem. Sometimes the leaves occur at the base of the plant (basal). Some leaves do not have a leafstalk and clasp the stem at their base (clasping). In other cases, the stem appears to pass through the base of the leaf (perfoliate).

Using these five steps (color, size, shape, leaves and leaf attachment) will help you gather the clues needed to quickly and easily identify the common wildflowers of Florida.

USING THE ICONS

Sometimes the botanical terms for leaf type, attachment and type of flower can be confusing and difficult to remember. Because of this, we have included icons at the bottom of each page. They can be used to quickly and visually match the main features of the plant to the specimen you are viewing without needing to completely understand the botanical terms. By using the photos, text descriptions and icons in this field guide, you should be able to quickly and easily identify most of the common wildflowers of Florida.

The icons are arranged from left to right in the following order: flower cluster type, flower type, leaf type, leaf attachment and fruit. The first two flower icons refer to cluster type and flower type. While these are not botanically separate categories, we have made separate icons for them to simplify identification.

FLOWER CLUSTER ICONS

Flat

Round

Spike

(icon color is dependent on flower color)

Clusters (collections) of flowers can be categorized into one of three cluster types based on its overall shape. The flat, round and spike types refer to the cluster shape, which is easy to observe. Technically, there is another cluster type, composite, which appears as a single daisy-like flower, but is actually a cluster of many tiny flowers. Because this is often perceived as a flower type, we have included the icon in the flower type section. See page 9 for its description.

Some examples of cluster types

Flat

Round

Spike

FLOWER TYPE ICONS

     (icon color is dependent on flower color)

Regular   **Irregular**   **Composite**   **Bell**   **Tube**

Botanically speaking, there are many types of flowers, but in this guide, we are simplifying them to five basic types. Regular flowers are defined as having a round shape with three or more petals, lacking a disk-like center. Irregular flowers are not round, but uniquely shaped with fused petals. Bell flowers are hanging with fused petals. Tube flowers are longer and narrower than bell flowers and point up. Composite flowers (technically a flower cluster) are usually compact round clusters of tiny flowers appearing as one larger flower.

Some examples of flower types

Regular   Irregular   Bell

Tube   Composite

disk flowers
ray flowers

Composite cluster: Although a composite flower is technically a type of flower cluster, we are including the icon in the flower type category, since most people unfamiliar with botany would see it as a separate flower type. A composite flower consists of petals (ray flowers) and/or a round disk-like center (disk flowers). Sometimes a composite has only ray flowers, sometimes only disk flowers, or both.

LEAF TYPE ICONS

 Simple   **Simple Lobed**   **Compound**   **Twice Compound**   **Palmate** **Spines**

Leaf type can be broken down into two main types: simple and compound. Simple leaves are leaves that are in one piece; the leaf is not divided into smaller leaflets. It can have teeth or be smooth along the edges. The simple leaf is depicted by the simple icon. Simple leaves may have lobes and sinuses that give the leaf a unique shape. These simple leaves with lobes are depicted by the simple lobed icon.

Some examples of leaf types

Simple   Simple Lobed   Compound

Twice Compound   Palmate   Spines

Compound leaves have two or more distinct small leaves, called leaflets, arising from a single stalk. In this book we are dividing compound leaves into regular compound, twice compound or palmate compound leaves. Twice compound leaves are those with many distinct leaflets that arise from a secondary leafstalk. Palmate compound leaves are those with three or more leaflets arising from a common central point. Cactus spines are depicted by the spine icon as a leaf type.

LEAF ATTACHMENT ICONS

Alternate **Opposite** **Whorl** **Perfoliate** **Clasping** **Basal**

Leaves attach to the stems in different ways for different plants. Check to see where and how each leaf is attached to the main stem. There are six main types of attachment, as indicated, but sometimes a plant can have two different types of attachments. This is most often seen in the combination of basal leaves and leaves that attach along the main stem (cauline leaves), either alternate or opposite. These wildflowers have some leaves at the base of the plant, usually in a rosette pattern, and some leaves along the stem. In these cases, both icons are presented. For most plants there will only be one leaf attachment icon.

Some examples of leaf attachment

Alternate   Opposite   Whorl

Perfoliate   Clasping   Basal

Alternate leaves attach to the stem in an alternating pattern, while opposite leaves attach to the stem directly opposite from each other. Whorled leaves have three or more leaves that attach around the stem at the same point. Perfoliate leaves are also stalkless and have a leaf base that completely surrounds the main stem. Clasping leaves have no stalk, and the base of the leaf partly surrounds the main stem. Basal leaves are those that originate at the base of a plant, near the ground, usually grouped in a round rosette.

11

FRUIT ICONS

   (icon color is dependent on fruit color at maturity)

Berry   **Pod**

In some flower descriptions a fruit category has been included. This may be especially useful when a plant is not in bloom or when the fruit is particularly large or otherwise noteworthy. Botanically speaking, there are many types of fruit. We have simplified these often confusing fruit categories into two general groups, berry and pod.

Some examples of fruit types

Berry   Pod

The berry icon is used to depict a soft, fleshy, often round structure containing seeds. The pod icon is used to represent a dry structure that, when mature, splits open to release seeds.

SEASON OF BLOOM

Most wildflowers have a specific season of blooming. You probably won't see, for example, the common spring-blooming Lady Lupine blooming in summer or fall. Knowing the season of bloom can help you narrow your selection as you try to identify an unknown flower. In this field guide, spring usually refers to early February, March, April and the first half of May, although several flowers, including Annual Phlox, bloom as early as January in some areas of the state. Summer means late May, June, July and August. Fall usually means September, October, and the first half of November. Late November, December and January are considered winter.

LIFE CYCLE/ORIGIN

The life cycle of a wildflower describes how long a wildflower lives. Annual wildflowers are short-lived. They sprout, grow and bloom in only one season, never to return except from seed. Most wildflowers have perennial life cycles that last many years. Perennial wildflowers are usually deeply rooted plants that grow from the roots each year. They return each year from their roots, but they also produce seeds to start other perennial plants. Similar to the annual life cycle is the biennial life cycle. This group of plants takes two seasons of growth to bloom. In the first year, the plant produces a low growth of basal leaves. During the second year, the plant sends up a flower stalk from which it produces seeds for starting new plants. However, the original plant will not return for a third year of growth.

Origin indicates whether the plants are native or non-native. Most of the wildflowers in this book originate in Florida and are considered native plants. Non-native plants were often introduced unintentionally when they escaped from gardens or farms. The non-native plants in this book are now naturalized in Florida.

HABITATS

Some wildflowers thrive only in specific habitats. They may require certain types of soil, moisture, pH levels, fungi or nutrients. Other wildflowers are generalists and can grow almost anywhere. Sometimes noting the habitat surrounding a flower in question can be a clue to its identity.

RANGE

The wide variety of habitats in Florida naturally restricts the range of certain wildflowers that have specific requirements. Sometimes this section can help you eliminate a wildflower from consideration based solely on its range. However, please keep in mind that the ranges indicate where the flower is most commonly found. They are general guidelines only and there will certainly be exceptions to these ranges.

NOTES

The Notes are fun and fact-filled with many gee-whiz tidbits of interesting information such as historical uses, other common names, insect relationship, color variations and much more. Much of the information in this section cannot be found in other wildflower field guides.

CAUTION

In the Notes, it is mentioned that in some cultures, some of the wildflowers were used for medicine or food. While some find this interesting, DO NOT use this guide to identify edible or medicinal plants. Some of the wildflowers in Florida are toxic or have toxic look-alikes that can cause severe problems. Do not take the chance of making a mistake. Please enjoy the wildflowers with your eyes or camera. In addition, please don't pick, trample or transplant any wildflowers you see. The flower of a plant is its reproductive structure, and if you pick a flower, you have eliminated its ability to reproduce. Transplanting wildflowers is another destructive occurrence. Most wildflowers need specific soil types, pH levels or special bacteria or fungi in the soil to grow properly. If you attempt to transplant a wildflower to a habitat that is not suitable for its particular needs, the wildflower most likely will die. Also, some wildflowers, due to their dwindling populations, are protected by laws that forbid you to disturb them. Many Florida wildflowers are now available at local garden centers. These wildflowers have been cultivated and have not been dug from the wild. More gardeners are taking advantage of the availability of these wildflowers, planting native species and helping the planet.

Enjoy the Wild Wildflowers!

Jaret and Stan

COMMON NAME
Color indicator
Scientific name

Family: common family name (scientific family name)

Height: average range of mature plant; may indicate whether a shrub or vine

Flower: general information such as color, size of flower or flower cluster, may include flower type, number of petals or description of flower stem

Leaf: general description, may include shape, size, color, lobes, leaflets, teeth, veins, spines, attachment, leafstalk or description of plant stem

Fruit: berry or pod, may include shape, color or size

Bloom: season(s) or time of year when flower blooms

Cycle/Origin: annual, perennial, biennial; native or non-native

Habitat: examples of places where found, may include soil types or sun/shade preferences

Range: throughout or part of Florida where found

Notes: Helpful identification information, history, origin and other interesting gee-whiz nature facts.

**Not all icons are found on every page.
See preceding pages for icon descriptions.**

CLUSTER TYPE	FLOWER TYPE	LEAF TYPE	LEAF ATTACHMENT	FRUIT
Spike	Regular	Simple	Alternate	Berry

NARROWLEAF BLUE-EYED GRASS
Sisyrinchium angustifolium

Family: Iris (Iridaceae)

Height: 6-24" (15-61 cm)

Flower: collection of small blue flowers with bright yellow centers; each flower, ½-¾" (1-2 cm) wide, has 6 petals, each tipped with a tiny point; each flower group rises from a short stalk, which in turn comes from a longer leaf-like stem

Leaf: thin pointed grass-like leaves, ¼" (.6 cm) wide, and 8-20" (20-50 cm) long, are often confused with blades of grass

Fruit: small round green pod, ¼" (.6 cm) wide, turning dark brown at maturity

Bloom: spring, summer

Cycle/Origin: perennial; native

Habitat: moist soils, pinelands, open woods, roadside ditches, meadows

Range: throughout

Notes: Of the five species of blue-eyed grass in Florida, this plant is the most common. Often confused with tufts of grass, it is actually a member of the Iris family. Has fibrous vertical roots, unlike more common irises that spread on horizontal stems (rhizomes). Like other irises, this flower is made up of three petal-like sepals and three petals, all of which are shallowly notched and have tiny tips. Stems can sometimes be bluish purple.

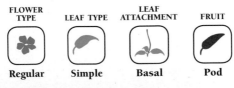

FLOWER TYPE	LEAF TYPE	LEAF ATTACHMENT	FRUIT
Regular	Simple	Basal	Pod

CLIMBING DAYFLOWER
Commelina diffusa

Family: Spiderwort (Commelinaceae)

Height: 6-24" (15-61 cm)

Flower: small solitary flower, ¾-1" (2-2.5 cm) wide, has 3 broad blue petals; upper 2 petals are slightly larger than lower petal; flower emerges from a green tubular bract

Leaf: lance-shaped leaves, 1-5" (2.5-13 cm) long, are shiny and smooth; alternately attached to and clasping a slender smooth creeping stem

Bloom: year-round

Cycle/Origin: perennial; non-native

Habitat: moist woods or disturbed sites, yards, wet ditches

Range: throughout

Notes: One of eight species of *Commelina* found in Florida, this wildflower occurs throughout subtropical and tropical regions of the world. Introduced into the Southeast, it is a common weed of moist habitats including lawns and gardens. A widely branching, often mat-forming plant that grows along the ground and roots at the stem nodes, thus it is also known as Creeping Dayflower. The small, bright blue flowers last for only one day. An extract from the petals has been used as an indigo dye for painting. Whitemouth Dayflower (*C. erecta*) (not shown) is an equally common Florida native with large, showier, pale blue upper petals and a much smaller lower petal that is white.

FLOWER TYPE	LEAF TYPE	LEAF ATTACHMENT	LEAF ATTACHMENT
Irregular	**Simple**	**Alternate**	**Clasping**

COMMON BLUE VIOLET
Viola sororia

Family: Violet (Violaceae)

Height: 4-10" (10-25 cm)

Flower: dark blue-to-deep violet (can be lavender or white) flower, 1" (2.5 cm) wide, with 5 distinct petals; center of flower is white and the 3 lower petals are strongly veined; flowers are usually below the leaves and found on their own flower stalks

Leaf: characteristic heart-shaped leaves with scalloped teeth; surface of leaf is often woolly and rolled along the edge; each leaf rises from the base of plant on its own woolly leafstalk

Bloom: spring

Cycle/Origin: perennial; native

Habitat: wet or moist woodlands, forest edges, disturbed soils

Range: throughout

Notes: Nearly 80 distinct species of violet in North America and over 900 worldwide. This is Florida's most abundant violet. Like all violets, its flower color is highly variable. Looks very similar to other species of blue violet. Many violet species are now lumped together under the species name *sororia*. Closely related to the pansy, a common garden annual. Often "pops up" in shady gardens and in lawns. Spreads mostly by underground runners, but also produces a seedpod with many tiny brown seeds. The leaves are high in vitamins and have been eaten raw or cooked.

FLOWER TYPE	LEAF TYPE	LEAF ATTACHMENT
Irregular	**Simple**	**Basal**

SPIDERWORT
Tradescantia ohiensis

Family: Spiderwort (Commelinaceae)

Height: 10-24" (25-61 cm)

Flower: cluster of up to 10 flowers, opening only a few at a time; each flower, 1-2" (2.5-5 cm) wide, with 3 blue-to-rose petals surrounding a golden yellow center; flowers are sometimes pink to white

Leaf: long grass-like leaves, 15" (38 cm) long, clasp the stem; each leaf is folded lengthwise, forming a V-shaped groove

Bloom: spring, summer

Cycle/Origin: perennial; native

Habitat: wet to dry sites, woodland margins, fields, meadows

Range: northern and central Florida

Notes: This unusual-looking plant with exotic-looking flowers is one of nine species of spiderwort in Florida. The flowers open in the morning and often wilt by noon on hot days. "Spider" in the common name may refer to its mucilaginous sap, which strings out like a spider's web when a leaf is torn. It is also said that the plant's jointed stems appear like a giant spider's legs. "Wort" is derived from *wyrt*, an Old English word for "plant." The genus name *Tradescantia* is in honor of J. Tradescant, an English gardener. It is an excellent but underutilized garden plant.

FLOWER TYPE	LEAF TYPE	LEAF ATTACHMENT	LEAF ATTACHMENT
Regular	**Simple**	**Alternate**	**Clasping**

OCEAN BLUE MORNING GLORY
Ipomoea indica

Family: Morning Glory (Convolvulaceae)

Height: 10-25' (3-7.6 m); vine

Flower: large blue-to-purplish blue flower, 2-3¼" (5-8 cm) wide, with a pale center and hairy petal-like sepals; 5 petals fused together to form a funnel-shaped flower

Leaf: variable-shaped leaves, 2-4" (5-10 cm) long, from heart-shaped to 3-lobed, stalked and hairy; alternately attached to a finely haired stem

Fruit: round green capsule, turning brown at maturity

Bloom: year-round

Cycle/Origin: perennial; native

Habitat: hammocks, disturbed areas, roadsides, old fields

Range: southern two-thirds of Florida

Notes: One of several very showy morning glory species found in Florida, the lovely blue-to-purplish blue flowers of this native vine indeed resemble the color of scenic Caribbean waters. An effective invader of open sunny sites, including forest margins, rights-of-way and recently disturbed locations, it quickly rambles over weedy vegetation and is capable of forming a dense ground cover. Although mostly distributed throughout much of the peninsula, it can sporadically be found in several panhandle counties.

FLOWER TYPE	LEAF TYPE	LEAF TYPE	LEAF ATTACHMENT	FRUIT
Tube	Simple	Simple Lobed	Alternate	Pod

FRAGRANT ERYNGO
Eryngium aromaticum

Family: Carrot (Apiaceae)

Height: 3-24" (7.5-61 cm)

Flower: small compact round flower head, ¼-¾" (.6-2 cm) wide, composed of numerous tiny, blue-to-white flowers; each flower has 5 petals; flower heads are backed by prickly bracts and persist on the plant after blooming

Leaf: grayish green-to-green leaves, deeply cut into 5 very narrow, lance-shaped lobes; alternately attached to a reclining or ascending stem

Bloom: summer, fall

Cycle/Origin: perennial; native

Habitat: dry sandy soils, pinelands, scrub areas

Range: throughout

Notes: Fragrant Eryngo is a charming but easy-to-overlook, low-growing perennial. The small, sharp-tipped leaves are inconspicuous most of the year, but densely cover the long flower stalks that appear in summer and autumn. Leaf-laden stalks sprawl along the ground or weakly rise and bear numerous grayish green flower heads that explode into bloom with tiny blue flowers. As "Fragrant" in the common name and the species name *aromaticum* imply, the flowers and the crushed leaves do have a pleasant odor.

CLUSTER TYPE	FLOWER TYPE	LEAF TYPE	LEAF ATTACHMENT
Round	**Regular**	**Simple Lobed**	**Alternate**

SKYFLOWER
Hydrolea corymbosa

Family: Waterleaf (Hydrophyllaceae)

Height: 8-24" (20-61 cm)

Flower: flat cluster, 1-3" (2.5-7.5 cm) wide, of several blue flowers, each ¾-1" (2-2.5 cm) wide, with 5 oval petals; cluster at the end of stem

Leaf: elliptical to lance-shaped leaves, 1-2¼" (2.5-5.5 cm) long, are stalked, have smooth edges and are alternately attached to an upright smooth stem

Bloom: spring, summer, fall

Cycle/Origin: perennial; native

Habitat: marshes, wet roadside ditches

Range: throughout

Notes: The lovely blue flowers of this eye-catching native of the Southeast truly mirror the color of a sun-quenched cloudless sky, earning its common name. The plants frequently occur in wet ditches along roads, and although small in stature, the blooms are noticeable even by those travelling at highway speeds. Species name *corymbosa* refers to the plant's flat-topped flower cluster, known as a corymb. A wetland indicator plant and the most common member of the genus *Hydrolea* in Florida.

CLUSTER TYPE

Flat

FLOWER TYPE

Regular

LEAF TYPE

Simple

LEAF ATTACHMENT

Alternate

WILD BLUE PHLOX
Phlox divaricata

Family: Phlox (Polemoniaceae)

Height: 10-20" (25-50 cm)

Flower: loose flat cluster, 2-3" (5-7.5 cm) wide, of pale blue flowers; each flower, 1" (2.5 cm) wide, made up of 5 petals fused together at their bases into a short tube

Leaf: toothless lance-shaped leaves, 1-2" (2.5-5 cm) long, are stalkless and oppositely attached along the stem

Bloom: winter, spring

Cycle/Origin: perennial; native

Habitat: rich woodlands, open forests, partial shade

Range: northern Florida

Notes: Wild Blue Phlox is a single-stemmed woodland wildflower that grows in the dappled sunlight of forest floors. Also called Wood Phlox or Blue Phlox. Its fragrant flowers are occasionally white or dark blue, with stems often hairy and sticky to the touch. The closed flower buds have twisted petals appearing like a torch, hence the name *Phlox*, Greek for "flame." Species name *divaricata* means "to spread," referring to the plant's sprawling and patch-forming growth habit. Although mostly limited in the wild to the Florida panhandle, it is widely cultivated and readily available for purchase. Closely related to garden phlox. Blooms in late winter and continues through much of the spring in Florida. In bygone years, was often picked to add to wildflower bouquets for mothers on Mother's Day.

CLUSTER TYPE	FLOWER TYPE	LEAF TYPE	LEAF ATTACHMENT
Flat	Regular	Simple	Opposite

BLUE MISTFLOWER
Conoclinium coelestinum

Family: Aster (Asteraceae)

Height: 12-36" (30-91 cm)

Flower: fuzzy flat cluster, 1½-4" (4-10 cm) wide, of many purplish blue flower heads, each with 35-70 disk flowers, but lacking petals (ray flowers)

Leaf: triangular to lance-shaped leaves, 1½-5" (4-13 cm) long, are highly textured, have toothed margins and are oppositely attached to an upright, hairy, green-to-reddish green stem

Bloom: year-round

Cycle/Origin: perennial; native

Habitat: moist soils, wet meadows, roadside ditches, pond margins, woodland edges, disturbed sites

Range: throughout

Notes: Formerly in the genus *Eupatorium*, Blue Mistflower is now recognized as one of three species in the genus *Conoclinium*, which in the United States occurs only in the eastern part of the country. Also called Wild Ageratum, named in part for the similar-looking common garden annual. Species name *coelestinum* means "sky blue," referring to the color of the fuzzy flower heads. Despite this reference, the actual bloom color is variable, from pinkish blue to lilac to reddish purple to violet. Spreads rapidly by creeping stems (rhizomes) and can form extensive colonies. It has a long history of medicinal uses such as treatments for colds and coughs.

CLUSTER TYPE	FLOWER TYPE	LEAF TYPE	LEAF ATTACHMENT
Flat	**Composite**	**Simple**	**Opposite**

WILD LUPINE
Lupinus perennis

Family: Pea or Bean (Fabaceae)

Height: 12-24" (30-61 cm)

Flower: spike cluster, 3-7" (7.5-18 cm) long, of pea-like blue flowers; each flower, ⅝" (1.6 cm) wide; what appears to be 3 petals (called, from the top down, standard, wing and keel) are actually 5 petals fused together

Leaf: leafstalks arise from the base of plant and end with palmate leaves, 5-10" (13-25 cm) wide, that are made up of 7-11 small leaflets

Fruit: fuzzy green fruit, up to 2" (5 cm) long, shaped like a pea pod, turns black with age, contains 10-20 small brown-to-black seeds; many fruits per plant

Bloom: spring

Cycle/Origin: perennial; native

Habitat: dry sandy soils in open woods, sandhills

Range: northern Florida

Notes: Like other legumes, this delicate, cool-season wildflower fixes nitrogen from the air into the soil, improving soil fertility. A plant that establishes itself early (and often more densely) on sites that are regularly disturbed, it prefers open sandy locations. Natural or prescribed fire is important to help maintain such open habitat conditions. The only Florida host for Frosted Elfin, an imperiled and declining butterfly found only in a few scattered northern counties. All parts of the plant, but especially the seeds, are poisonous.

CLUSTER TYPE	FLOWER TYPE	LEAF TYPE	LEAF ATTACHMENT	FRUIT
Spike	Irregular	Palmate	Basal	Pod

PICKERELWEED
Pontederia cordata

Family: Pickerelweed (Pontederiaceae)

Height: aquatic

Flower: many spike clusters, 4-6" (10-15 cm) long, of small blue flowers; each flower, ½" (1 cm) long, has 3 upper petals (middle upper petal has 2 small yellow spots) and 3 lower petals

Leaf: pointed, toothless, heart-shaped to narrow leaves, 4-10" (10-25 cm) long, arise from an underwater root; each leaf is indented at the base where the leafstalk attaches

Bloom: year-round

Cycle/Origin: perennial; native

Habitat: shallow lake margins, wetlands, ponds, streams

Range: throughout

Notes: An attractive marginal aquatic plant, Pickerelweed spreads by underground stems (rhizomes) and often forms large stands. Found in shallow wetlands or periodically flooded sites, its leaves and flowers rise above the water, but are unable to tolerate submersion. The common name refers to pickerel, a type of fish that shares a similar watery habitat. While its colorful blue flowers are produced throughout the year in southern Florida, the plant goes dormant during the cooler winter months in the northern counties. Easily grown as an ornamental, it is one of the most common aquatic plants in cultivation.

CLUSTER TYPE	FLOWER TYPE	LEAF TYPE	LEAF ATTACHMENT
Spike	**Irregular**	**Simple**	**Basal**

CANADA TOADFLAX
Nuttallanthus canadensis

Family: Snapdragon (Scrophulariaceae)

Height: 6-24" (15-61 cm)

Flower: loose spike cluster, 2½-8" (6-20 cm) long, of blue-to-violet flowers; each flower, ½" (1 cm) long, is made up of 2 lips; 2-lobed upper lip is upright, 3-lobed lower lip has a raised white center and a downward-projecting slender spur

Leaf: small thin smooth leaves, ¼-1¼" (.6-3 cm) long, alternately attached to a slender upright stem; a series of sprawling stems at the base form a distinct rosette; leaves on the prostrate stems are opposite

Bloom: winter, early spring

Cycle/Origin: annual, biennial; native

Habitat: fields, roadsides, disturbed sites, fallow agricultural lands

Range: throughout

Notes: A delicate-looking wildflower, Canada Toadflax is an early spring invader of sunny disturbed areas with sandy soils. The slender wispy stems support a loose bouquet of small flowers that often can, by their sheer density, turn roadsides and fields into a sea of blue. This plant is a preferred host of Common Buckeye butterfly caterpillars. The genus name pays tribute to Thomas Nuttall, a noted naturalist who led several scientific expeditions throughout North America during the early 1800s.

CLUSTER TYPE	FLOWER TYPE	LEAF TYPE	LEAF ATTACHMENT	LEAF ATTACHMENT
Spike	**Irregular**	**Simple**	**Alternate**	**Opposite**

BLUE PORTERWEED
Stachytarpheta jamaicensis

Family: Verbena (Verbenaceae)

Height: 12-24" (30-61 cm)

Flower: long stout spike cluster, 6-18" (15-45 cm) long, of widely flaring tubular flowers of blue-violet with white centers; cluster is at the end of stem and blooms from the base of spike upward, with only a few flowers opening at a time

Leaf: oval leaves, ¾-4" (2-10 cm) long, with coarsely toothed margins; oppositely attached to an ascending stem

Bloom: year-round

Cycle/Origin: perennial; native

Habitat: disturbed sites, forest margins

Range: southern Florida

Notes: This low-grower produces broadly spreading clumps that are much wider than they are tall. Although considered Florida's only native porterweed and despite the species name *jamaicensis*, some botanists think the plant was actually introduced from the Bahamas by early settlers. Genus name *Stachytarpheta* is from Greek words that combine to mean "thick spike," aptly describing the cluster shape. Blue Porterweed makes a good garden plant and attracts many species of butterflies and hummingbirds. Often confused with the taller, upright-growing Nettleleaf Velvetberry (*S. urticufolia*) (not shown), a non-native cultivated plant widely available for purchase.

CLUSTER TYPE	FLOWER TYPE	LEAF TYPE	LEAF ATTACHMENT
Spike	**Tube**	**Simple**	**Opposite**

AZURE BLUE SAGE
Salvia azurea

Family: Mint (Lamiaceae)

Height: 2-4' (61-122 cm)

Flower: elongated spike cluster, 6-18" (15-45 cm) long, composed of whorls of up to 4 bright blue (occasionally white) flowers; each flower, ½-¾" (1-2 cm) long, has petals fused to form a long tube with an upper lip and a longer 2-lobed lower lip

Leaf: elliptical to uniformly thin leaves, 2-4" (5-10 cm) long, with toothed margins, oppositely attached to a slender hairy upright stem

Fruit: 4 small brown nutlets in an elongated brown pod that is open and cup-shaped

Bloom: summer, fall

Cycle/Origin: perennial; native

Habitat: pinelands, dry woods

Range: northern and central Florida

Notes: The species name *azurea* means "sky blue" and refers to the plant's vibrant flower color. Unlike Lyreleaf Sage (pg. 161), which has basal leaves, Azure Blue Sage lacks leaves at the plant base. Found in the wild in dry pine-dominated woodlands. A clump-forming perennial, it is easily grown from seed and a welcome addition to any garden. Although drought tolerant once established, it does benefit from regular moisture. The flowers on the long spikes provide abundant nectar for butterflies, bees and hummingbirds.

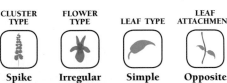

CLUSTER TYPE	FLOWER TYPE	LEAF TYPE	LEAF ATTACHMENT	FRUIT
Spike	Irregular	Simple	Opposite	Pod

RAYLESS SUNFLOWER
Helianthus radula

Family: Aster (Asteraceae)

Height: 24-36" (61-91 cm)

Flower: dark brown-to-reddish purple flower head, ½-1¼" (1-3 cm) wide, composed of numerous ray flowers (petals lacking); ray flowers have noticeable, bright yellow flower parts (anthers)

Leaf: oval to elliptical basal leaves, 1½-5" (4-13 cm) long, occurring in a rosette; stem leaves (if present) are much smaller and oppositely attached to a rigid upright stem

Bloom: fall

Cycle/Origin: perennial; native

Habitat: moist pinelands, wet roadside ditches, disturbed sites

Range: northern and central Florida

Notes: Native to the Southeast, this odd-looking wildflower is one of the most distinctive and easily identifiable sunflowers in Florida since it lacks the large and showy yellow petals typical of other members of the genus. At first glance, the round, button-like brown flower heads resemble old dried blooms. However, upon closer inspection, the bright yellow anthers protruding from the numerous tiny disk flowers are quite evident (see inset). The plant often forms extensive dense colonies in moist pinelands or along wet roadways.

FLOWER TYPE	LEAF TYPE	LEAF ATTACHMENT	LEAF ATTACHMENT
Composite	**Simple**	**Opposite**	**Basal**

fruit

CORKYSTEM PASSIONFLOWER
Passiflora suberosa

Family: Passionflower (Passifloraceae)

Height: 4-8' (1.2-2.4 m); vine

Flower: intricate, pale green flower, ¼-½" (.6-1 cm) wide, with 5 elliptical sepals below a whorl of short, green-to-white filaments around a greenish white center bearing 5 large flower parts; single flowers or in pairs

Leaf: extremely variable-shaped leaves, uniformly thin to elliptical or lobed, ½-4" (1-10 cm) long; twining tendril from leaf attachments

Fruit: smooth oval green berry, ¼" (.6 cm) long, ripening to dark purple

Bloom: year-round

Cycle/Origin: perennial; native

Habitat: hammocks, coastal areas

Range: southern half of Florida

Notes: A wide-ranging tropical vine found from South America to Florida. Highly drought and salt tolerant, it handles the harsh conditions of coastal habitats with ease, but is much less amenable to freezing temperatures. The first part of the common name refers to the conspicuous, corky bark on the older, lower stems. A welcome addition to any landscape as a ground cover or low climber, it also serves as the host for Gulf Fritillary, Zebra Longwing and Julia butterfly caterpillars. As a result, it has become a staple component of southern Florida butterfly gardens.

FLOWER TYPE	LEAF TYPE	LEAF TYPE	LEAF ATTACHMENT	FRUIT
Regular	**Simple**	**Simple Lobed**	**Alternate**	**Berry**

INDIAN BLANKET
Gaillardia pulchella

Family: Aster (Asteraceae)

Height: 8-30" (20-76 cm)

Flower: large daisy-like flower head, 2-3" (5-7.5 cm) wide, composed of many yellow-tipped orange, crimson or purple petals (ray flowers) surrounding a reddish purple center (disk flowers)

Leaf: hairy lance-shaped leaves, ½-4" (1-10 cm) long; lower leaves longer and toothed or lobed; upper leaves shorter and clasping; leaves are alternately attached to an upright, slender, hairy, sticky stem

Bloom: year-round

Cycle/Origin: annual, perennial; native

Habitat: dry disturbed areas, along roads, fields, dunes, coastal sites

Range: throughout

Notes: Aptly named, Indian Blanket is one of the state's most brilliantly colored, showy wildflowers. Not surprisingly, it is also one of the most popular of Florida's native plants and is readily available for purchase. Easy to grow, virtually maintenance free and exceptionally tolerant of poor dry soils. Thus, it is commonly planted along highways and other rights-of-way. Although only an annual or short-lived perennial, it readily self-seeds, providing a lasting display year after year.

FLOWER TYPE	LEAF TYPE	LEAF TYPE	LEAF ATTACHMENT	LEAF ATTACHMENT
Composite	**Simple**	**Simple Lobed**	**Alternate**	**Clasping**

FEW-FLOWERED MILKWEED
Asclepias lanceolata

Family: Milkweed (Asclepiadaceae)

Height: 3-5' (.9-1.5 m)

Flower: small domed flat cluster, 1-2" (2.5-5 cm) wide, of several bright flowers; each flower, ¼" (.6 cm) wide, with 5 downward-curving red petals and a deeply divided orange crown

Leaf: long narrow lance-shaped leaves, 2-9½" (5-24 cm) long; the few leaves are widely spaced along a tall thin unbranched stem

Fruit: elongated curved green pod, 3½-4½" (9-11 cm) long, narrow, tapering toward tip; turns brown with age, splitting open along 1 side; dark brown seeds with cottony fuzz are carried away by wind

Bloom: summer, fall

Cycle/Origin: perennial; native

Habitat: marshes, swamps, wet areas, ditches

Range: throughout

Notes: A tall plant with bright compact clusters (made up of a few orange and red flowers) that protrude above surrounding vegetation and make the plant easy to spot even from afar, despite its spindly stem. Like most other milkweeds, its stem and leaves contain a thick milky sap and toxic cardiac glycosides. Monarch butterfly caterpillars use these poisons to gain protection from predators.

CLUSTER TYPE	FLOWER TYPE	LEAF TYPE	LEAF ATTACHMENT	FRUIT
Flat	Irregular	Simple	Opposite	Pod

fruit

BUTTERFLYWEED
Asclepias tuberosa

Family: Milkweed (Asclepiadaceae)

Height: 12-24" (30-61 cm)

Flower: large flat-topped cluster, 2-3" (5-7.5 cm) wide, of small orange flowers, ⅜" (.9 cm) wide; each flower has downward-curving petals

Leaf: toothless hairy leaves, 2-6" (5-15 cm) long, that widen near their tips

Fruit: upright small clusters of narrow pods, 6" (15 cm) long, covered with fine hairs; pods contain large brown seeds with silken "parachutes" to carry away each seed

Bloom: spring, summer

Cycle/Origin: perennial; native

Habitat: dry sunny sites, sandy roadsides, open woodlands, pinelands

Range: throughout, except in extreme southern Florida

Notes: Found in dry open woodlands and at sandy roadsides, this true milkweed lacks milky sap; instead, its stem and leaves bleed clear sap. Species name *tuberosa* refers to its large vertical root (taproot), which makes it nearly impossible to transplant. However, it can be grown from seed. Its single stem branches only near the top and its flower stalks harbor up to 25 individual flowers. The bright orange flowers are a favorite of many insect pollinators, while the leaves serve as food for Monarch and Queen butterfly caterpillars.

CLUSTER TYPE	FLOWER TYPE	LEAF TYPE	LEAF ATTACHMENT	FRUIT
Flat	Irregular	Simple	Alternate	Pod

SCARLET MILKWEED
Asclepias curassavica

Family: Milkweed (Asclepiadaceae)

Height: 12-36" (30-91 cm)

Flower: large domed flat cluster, 2-4" (5-10 cm) wide, of several small bright flowers; each flower, ¼" (.6 cm) wide, with downward-curving, scarlet-orange petals and a deeply divided, yellowish orange crown

Leaf: lance-shaped leaves, 3½-7" (9-18 cm) long, are uniformly thin and oppositely attached by short stalks to a smooth, unbranched or branched stem

Fruit: elongated narrow green pod, 2-4" (5-10 cm) long, tapering toward the tip; turns brown, opens to release numerous seeds with cottony tufts

Bloom: year-round

Cycle/Origin: perennial; non-native

Habitat: pastures, roadsides, disturbed sites

Range: central and southern Florida

Notes: Although similar to Few-flowered Milkweed (pg. 53), Scarlet Milkweed flowers appear more orange overall, and the plant is noticeably more compact, leafy and often multi-branched. A native of tropical America, this evergreen, frost-tender perennial is grown widely as a landscape ornamental. In fact, it has become the most commonly available milkweed for use in butterfly gardens. It has escaped cultivation and naturalized in portions of the Florida peninsula, where it is considered an invasive weed.

CLUSTER TYPE	FLOWER TYPE	LEAF TYPE	LEAF ATTACHMENT	FRUIT
Flat	Irregular	Simple	Opposite	Pod

fruit

FIREBUSH
Hamelia patens

Family: Madder (Rubiaceae)

Height: 4-15' (1.2-4.6 m); shrub

Flower: showy branched spike cluster, 2-7" (5-18 cm) long, of many 5-angled, orange-to-red tubular flowers; each flower, ½-1" (1-2.5 cm) long, on red stalk; clusters at ends of stems or from upper leaf attachments

Leaf: elliptical green leaves, 2-7" (5-18 cm) long, with red veins and smooth margins; stalked, attached oppositely or in whorls to upright, multi-branched, reddish green-to-reddish brown stem

Fruit: round green berry, ¼" (.6 cm) wide, ripens to black

Bloom: year-round

Cycle/Origin: perennial; native

Habitat: hammocks, coastal habitats

Range: central and southern Florida

Notes: A fast-growing, densely branched, woody shrub with showy clusters of bright orange-to-scarlet flowers that are a favorite of hummingbirds and butterflies alike. The resulting berries are edible and also relished by birds and small mammals. One of the most popular and widely available native plants for purchase in Florida. Easily cultivated in full sun to fairly deep shade. Historically, leaf extracts were applied to treat wounds and skin ailments, and consumed to alleviate fever, rheumatism and cholera. Such extracts have recently been shown to possess antibacterial and antifungal properties.

CLUSTER TYPE	FLOWER TYPE	LEAF TYPE	LEAF ATTACHMENT	LEAF ATTACHMENT	FRUIT
Spike	Tube	Simple	Opposite	Whorl	Berry

ORANGE AZALEA
Rhododendron austrinum

Family: Heath (Ericaceae)

Height: 6-15' (1.8-4.6 m); shrub

Flower: dense round cluster, 4-8" (10-20 cm) wide, of several fragrant, orange-to-bright yellow flowers, each 2-3" (1.5-7.6 cm) long, with 5 wavy petals fused at their bases, forming a tube and broadly flaring at the mouth; very long flower parts protrude from tube well beyond the mouth and curve upward at the tips

Leaf: hairy elliptical leaves, 1½-3½" (4-9 cm) long, on an upright, multi-branched, brown-to-gray stem

Fruit: reddish brown capsule, ½-¾" (1-2 cm) long, hairy, cylindrical, splits in late summer to release seeds

Bloom: early spring

Cycle/Origin: perennial; native

Habitat: moist acidic soils, floodplain forests with partial shade, stream banks

Range: northern Florida

Notes: Nondescript for most of the year, this deciduous woody shrub explodes in early spring with a truly show-stopping display of color. Vivid orange-to-bright yellow blooms make the bare branches appear as if on fire. Thus, also called Florida Flame Azalea. Limited almost exclusively in the wild to the panhandle, it is listed by the state of Florida as endangered. However, it is widely available for purchase. Nearly maintenance free if planted in moist acidic soil.

CLUSTER TYPE	FLOWER TYPE	LEAF TYPE	LEAF ATTACHMENT	FRUIT
Round	Tube	Simple	Alternate	Pod

fruit

DIXIE TICK TREFOIL
Desmodium tortuosum

Family: Pea or Bean (Fabaceae)

Height: 3-9' (.9-2.7 m)

Flower: loose (often branched) group of small pea-like flowers; each flower, ¼" (.6 cm) wide, has 2 lips and is pink with a white center; flowers on flower stalks at the end of stems or from upper leaf attachments

Leaf: compound leaves, with 3 elliptical leaflets, each 2½-4" (6-10 cm) long; leaflets rough and sticky above and below due to dense hooked stiff hairs; simple leaves sometimes on lower part of stout, upright, sticky, reddish green-to-green stem; leaves alternate

Fruit: hairy flat green pod, 1-1½" (2.5-4 cm) long, with 2-9 oval segments; pod turns brown and segments separate when mature

Bloom: year-round

Cycle/Origin: annual; non-native

Habitat: disturbed sites, roadsides, croplands, fields

Range: throughout

Notes: Produces a large amount of small, segmented, densely hairy pods that adhere tick-like to clothes, animal fur and feathers—a characteristic that gives this plant and others in *Desmodium* the tick trefoil name. Introduced from West Indies as a forage crop and to help improve soil structure, it has naturalized and is now a very invasive weed. Host for caterpillars of the migratory Long-tailed Skipper.

FLOWER TYPE	LEAF TYPE	LEAF TYPE	LEAF ATTACHMENT	FRUIT
Irregular	Simple	Compound	Alternate	Pod

EASTERN MILKPEA
Galactia regularis

Family: Pea or Bean (Fabaceae)

Height: 2-5' (61-152 cm); vine

Flower: small pea-like pink flowers, ⅕-½" (.8-1 cm) wide, borne in short few-flowered groups originating in the leaf attachments

Leaf: compound leaves, divided into 3 oval to elliptical leaflets; each leaflet, ½-1¾" (1-4.5 cm) long, with smooth margins; leaves alternately attached to a trailing stem

Fruit: flattened bean-like green pod, 1-1½" (2.5-4 cm) long, is hairy and turns brown at maturity

Bloom: spring, summer, fall

Cycle/Origin: perennial; native

Habitat: pinelands, forest margins, dry woods, fields

Range: throughout

Notes: Distinctive oval leaflets adorn the multi-branched stems of this mostly ground-hugging vine. In addition, a few small pink blossoms are sparsely spaced along the stem. Although "Milkpea" is in the common name, the stems have no milky sap. Genus name *Galactia*, derived from Greek and meaning "milk yielding," was erroneously applied to this plant when it was originally described. The seeds from Eastern Milkpea are enjoyed by songbirds and small mammals.

FLOWER TYPE	LEAF TYPE	LEAF ATTACHMENT	FRUIT
Irregular	**Compound**	**Alternate**	**Pod**

fruit

GARDEN VETCH
Vicia sativa

Family: Pea or Bean (Fabaceae)

Height: 10-36" (25-91 cm)

Flower: purplish pink-to-rose (can be white) flower, ½-⅔" (1-1.6 cm) long, on a very short flower stalk; flowers occur in pairs from upper leaf attachment (axis)

Leaf: compound leaves, 1¼-2¼" (3-5.5 cm) long, with 3-8 oblong leaflet pairs and a branched tendril at the tips of end leaflets; leaves alternately attached to an upright or reclining stem

Fruit: smooth flattened green pod, 1½-2½" (4-6 cm) long, turning black at maturity; splits open to release small round seeds

Bloom: spring, summer

Cycle/Origin: annual; non-native

Habitat: disturbed areas, roadsides, old fields, forest margins

Range: northern half of Florida

Notes: Also called Common or Narrowleaf Vetch, this spring or early summer legume is a frequent plant of roadsides, waste areas and other disturbed sites. Native to Europe, it is easily spread by seed and has naturalized throughout much of North America. The sprawling stems often form dense entanglements as the tendrils twine together or attach to neighboring vegetation.

FLOWER TYPE

Irregular

LEAF TYPE

Compound

LEAF ATTACHMENT

Alternate

FRUIT

Pod

PINK WOOD SORREL
Oxalis debilis

Family: Wood Sorrel (Oxalidaceae)

Height: 3-10" (7.5-25 cm)

Flower: small pink flower, ½-¾" (1-2 cm) long, with 5 petals fused at their bases and forming a funnel shape, has darker pink lines in the throat and a green center; flowers are borne on long flower stalks

Leaf: glossy clover-like compound leaves composed of 3 heart-shaped leaflets, each ¾-2½" (2-6 cm) wide; leaflets are attached at the tips; leaves appear to be on stems, but are actually on long leafstalks

Bloom: spring, summer, fall

Cycle/Origin: perennial; non-native

Habitat: wet sites, open woodlands, roadside ditches, forest margins

Range: throughout

Notes: A delicate plant that lacks stems, the large glossy leaves and bright pink flowers arise on long leafstalks and flower stalks. The leaves contain high levels of oxalates that give the foliage a sour taste when consumed. A shamrock look-alike, Pink Wood Sorrel grows as individual mounded plants in scattered small groupings in a variety of moist sites. Native to the American tropics, this weedy wildflower has naturalized throughout Florida and other parts of the Southeast. Although attractive, it is an invasive species that should not be planted in home landscapes.

FLOWER TYPE	LEAF TYPE	LEAF ATTACHMENT
Regular	**Compound**	**Basal**

NUTTALL THISTLE
Cirsium nuttallii

Family: Aster (Asteraceae)

Height: 3-10' (.9-3 m)

Flower: large rounded flower head, ½-1¼" (1-3 cm) wide, of pale pink-to-lavender-to-purple disk flowers (no ray flowers) sitting on a green base of tight bracts without long spines; heads atop single, nearly leafless long stalks; several flower heads per plant

Leaf: very spiny, deeply lobed, narrow to elliptical leaves, 4-10" (10-25 cm) long; basal leaves are longer and form a distinct rosette; the few stem leaves are alternate and clasp a smooth, often branched stem

Bloom: spring, summer, fall

Cycle/Origin: perennial; native

Habitat: roadsides, open fields, disturbed sites, pastures, moist pinelands

Range: throughout

Notes: A tall robust wildflower native to the Southeast. Although it appears similar to Purple Thistle (pg. 145), Nuttall Thistle is much more slender and has smaller heads with bracts that don't have long spines. However, the deeply lobed leaves are well armored, making Nuttall a formidable plant to handle or closely inspect. Showy, fuzzy-looking flower heads attract many pollinating insects. The species is named for English naturalist, botanist and painter Thomas Nuttall, who lived and traveled extensively in America in the early 1800s.

FLOWER TYPE	LEAF TYPE	LEAF ATTACHMENT	LEAF ATTACHMENT	LEAF ATTACHMENT
Composite	Simple Lobed	Alternate	Clasping	Basal

MARYLAND MEADOW BEAUTY
Rhexia mariana

Family: Meadow Beauty (Melastomataceae)

Height: 7-36" (18-91 cm)

Flower: large showy flower, 1-1½" (2.5-4 cm) wide, with 4 rose or pink (can be pale purple or white) petals and 8 large conspicuous flower parts (anthers) that are bright yellow to orangish yellow

Leaf: lance-shaped leaves, ¾-2½" (2-6 cm) long, are oppositely attached to an upright hairy stem

Bloom: spring, summer, fall

Cycle/Origin: perennial; native

Habitat: roadside ditches, moist pinelands, edges of marshes, low-lying fields

Range: throughout

Notes: Maryland Meadow Beauty is one of ten *Rhexia* species found in Florida. Also called Pale Meadow Beauty due to the wide variation of flower color, ranging from pink to pale purple to white. This lovely wildflower has lopsided petals that are extremely delicate and easily fall off when disturbed. Spreading readily by underground stems (rhizomes), the upright plants often form fairly extensive colonies in moist locations.

FLOWER TYPE	LEAF TYPE	LEAF ATTACHMENT
Regular	Simple	Opposite

ROSE-OF-PLYMOUTH
Sabatia stellaris

Family: Gentian (Gentianaceae)

Height: 6-20" (15-50 cm)

Flower: solitary showy flower, 1-1½" (2.5-4 cm) wide, composed of 5 oval pink petals (often fading to white) around a star-shaped yellow center or "eye" bordered in red; flower borne on a long slender flower stalk

Leaf: narrowly lance-shaped or elliptical leaves, 1-1½" (2.5-4 cm) long, tapering to a tip and oppositely attached; leaves are broader near the base of plant

Bloom: spring, summer, fall

Cycle/Origin: annual; native

Habitat: moist pinelands, wet ditches, coastal marshes, wet prairies

Range: throughout

Notes: This delicate annual is a diminutive, yet very showy wildflower of brackish coastal marshes and wet inland habitats. When encountered, Rose-of-Plymouth can be abundant, resulting in a landscape dotted with pink. The species name *stellaris* means "star-shaped" and refers to the shape of the center of the flower. "Plymouth" in the common name is for Plymouth, Massachusetts, where historically it was said to grow in abundance.

FLOWER TYPE	LEAF TYPE	LEAF ATTACHMENT
Regular	**Simple**	**Opposite**

CLIMBING ASTER
Ampelaster carolinianus

Family: Aster (Asteraceae)

Height: 4-15' (1.2-4.6 m)

Flower: small daisy-like flower head, 1-1½" (2.5-4 cm) wide, composed of numerous elongated pale pink-to-lavender petals (ray flowers) surrounding a reddish yellow center of disk flowers

Leaf: lance-shaped leaves, 1-4" (2.5-10 cm) long, with smooth margins; leaves are alternate and clasp a woody hairy multi-branched stem

Bloom: fall, winter

Cycle/Origin: perennial; native

Habitat: wet forests, stream banks, swamp margins, wet sites

Range: peninsular Florida

Notes: Climbing Aster behaves more like a vine than an upright perennial, although unlike a vine, which climbs upward or twines, the woody branching stems of this plant sprawl or scramble ("climb") over vegetation. It explodes into bloom very late in the season at a time when few other wildflowers are in flower, providing a bounty of nectar for butterflies and other insects. Despite occurring naturally in a variety of wet habitats, Climbing Aster adapts well to cultivation and is a unique addition to any native garden. The only species in the genus *Ampelaster*.

FLOWER TYPE	LEAF TYPE	LEAF ATTACHMENT	LEAF ATTACHMENT
Composite	Simple	Alternate	Clasping

MADAGASCAR PERIWINKLE
Catharanthus roseus

Family: Dogbane (Apocynaceae)

Height: 12-24" (30-61 cm)

Flower: large showy flower, 1-2" (2.5-5 cm) wide, is tubular with 5 broadly flaring pink or white petals around a dark pink center

Leaf: oval to elliptical, glossy leaves, 1-3½" (2.5-9 cm) long, are green, each with a pale greenish white central vein; leaves are evergreen and oppositely attached to an upright stem

Fruit: long cylindrical green pod, ¾-1½" (2-4 cm) long, turning brown at maturity; pods occur in pairs

Bloom: year-round

Cycle/Origin: perennial; non-native

Habitat: sunny open disturbed sites

Range: central and southern Florida

Notes: Although poisonous to people and livestock if eaten, Madagascar Periwinkle historically has been used medicinally, and currently its properties are of great interest in the medical community. Contains numerous alkaloids that have been shown to be useful in the treatment of many diseases including diabetes, malaria and various types of cancer. Commonly planted as a garden ornamental, it has escaped cultivation and is now widely naturalized throughout many tropical regions of the world. A perennial in warmer areas, but typically grown as an annual in cooler climates.

FLOWER TYPE	LEAF TYPE	LEAF ATTACHMENT	FRUIT
Regular	Simple	Opposite	Pod

SHOWY EVENING-PRIMROSE
Oenothera speciosa

Family: Evening-primrose (Onagraceae)

Height: 6-24" (15-61 cm)

Flower: large pink flower, 1½-3" (4-13 cm) wide, becoming white toward the yellow center, has 4 petals with darker pink veins and notched edges; a solitary flower is attached by a short flower stalk from upper leaf attachment (axis)

Leaf: uniformly thin or lance-shaped leaves, 1-3" (2.5-7.5 cm) long; edges shallowly toothed or deeply cut into narrow pointed lobes; multiple spreading, upward-arching stems

Fruit: narrow oval ridged pod, 1-2" (2.5-5 cm) long, is green, turning brown at maturity

Bloom: spring, summer

Cycle/Origin: perennial; non-native

Habitat: roadsides, old fields, disturbed sites

Range: northern and central Florida

Notes: The showy pink flowers are a departure from the more modest yellow blooms of other evening-primroses. Despite "Evening" in its common name and unlike others in the genus, its bowl-shaped flowers open in the morning and stay open until dark. Although popular for garden use, it spreads aggressively by creeping roots and can overtake small landscapes. Tolerant of poor soils and dry conditions, it has naturalized along sunny roads and other waste areas.

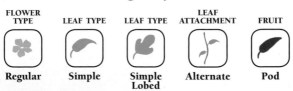

FLOWER TYPE	LEAF TYPE	LEAF TYPE	LEAF ATTACHMENT	FRUIT
Regular	Simple	Simple Lobed	Alternate	Pod

VIRGINIA SALT MARSH MALLOW
Kosteletzkya virginica

Family: Mallow (Malvaceae)

Height: 3-6' (.9-1.8 m)

Flower: large flower, 2-3" (5-7.5 cm) wide, with 5 broad, light pink petals around a column of bright yellow flower parts (stamens); flowers somewhat droop on flower stalks from the upper leaf attachments

Leaf: hairy triangular leaves, 3-7" (7.5-18 cm) long, with flared or slightly lobed bases; alternately attached with long leafstalks to upright multi-branched stem

Fruit: stiff-bristled, 5-angled green capsule, ½" (1 cm) wide, turns brown, has 5 smooth, dark brown seeds

Bloom: summer, fall

Cycle/Origin: perennial; native

Habitat: saltwater, brackish or freshwater marshes; swamps, wet ditches

Range: throughout

Notes: A many-flowered plant producing large, slightly drooping pink flowers that resemble common garden hibiscus blooms. Despite "Salt Marsh" in its common name, this tall, multi-branched plant also grows in freshwater marshes throughout Florida. Thrives in wet conditions in the wild, but it is easily grown and makes a showy addition to the home garden. The only downside is that each blossom lasts but a single day. Several cultivated varieties are available for purchase.

FLOWER TYPE	LEAF TYPE	LEAF ATTACHMENT	FRUIT
Regular	Simple	Alternate	Pod

RAILROADVINE
Ipomoea pes-caprae

Family: Morning Glory (Convolvulaceae)

Height: 10-20' (3-6.1 m); vine

Flower: usually solitary, large pink flower, 2-3" (5-7.5 cm) wide, has 5 petals fused to form a funnel shape and has a darker rose center with lines radiating outward

Leaf: large smooth oblong leaves, 2-4" (5-10 cm) long, are notched at the tips and alternately attached along a stout trailing branched stem

Fruit: round green capsule, turning brown at maturity, contains 4 large dark seeds

Bloom: spring, summer, fall; sometimes year-round

Cycle/Origin: perennial; native

Habitat: beach dunes, shorelines, disturbed sites

Range: coastal Florida

Notes: Railroadvine is a coastal plant and does not occur in inland Florida. This fast-growing "pioneer plant" colonizes barren areas just above the high tide line. A robust and evergreen ground cover that grows to a height of 2-5 inches (5-13 cm), but can ramble over large areas, thus helping to stabilize sand dunes and beaches. It is heat, salt and wind tolerant and will grow vigorously in poor soils. Has a large, penetrating, vertical root (taproot) and succulent stems that branch freely and root at the nodes. The buoyant seeds are carried on ocean currents, resulting in a very broad distribution in the tropics. May flower year-round in southern coastal areas of Florida.

FLOWER TYPE	LEAF TYPE	LEAF ATTACHMENT	FRUIT
Tube	**Simple**	**Alternate**	**Pod**

TALL ELEPHANT'S FOOT
Elephantopus elatus

Family: Aster (Asteraceae)

Height: 2-4' (61-122 cm)

Flower: compact flat clusters, ½-1" (1-2.5 cm) wide, of numerous purplish pink-to-nearly white disk flowers, lacking ray flowers; blooms open only a few at a time; 3 conspicuous, triangular, leaf-like green bracts immediately below the clusters; clusters are borne on widely branched, rough stalks

Leaf: broad basal leaves, 3-8" (7.5-20 cm) long, in a rosette, each with hairy, scalloped or toothed margins and tapering at the base; stem leaves are few, oval, reduced in size and alternately attached

Bloom: summer, fall

Cycle/Origin: perennial; native

Habitat: disturbed sites, roadsides, open woodlands, sandhills, pinelands

Range: throughout

Notes: This unusual-looking plant is a distinctive fall wildflower, common in open dry woodlands. The genus name *Elephantopus* refers to the prominent basal rosette of thick leaves that resembles (with some imagination) the rounded foot of an elephant, and the species name *elatus* means "lofty" or "high," referring to its tall growth habit. Despite being not overly showy, the small flowers are regularly visited by a wide variety of butterflies and other pollinating insects.

CLUSTER TYPE	FLOWER TYPE	LEAF TYPE	LEAF ATTACHMENT	LEAF ATTACHMENT
Flat	Composite	Simple	Alternate	Basal

TURKEY TANGLE FOGFRUIT
Phyla nodiflora

Family: Verbena (Verbenaceae)

Height: 4-12" (10-30 cm)

Flower: dense cylindrical spike cluster, ½-1" (1-2.5 cm) long, of whitish pink flowers with 5 petals; flowers bloom from bottom of spike upward; clusters at ends of long upright stalks

Leaf: thick, coarse, green-to-reddish green leaves, ¾-2" (2-5 cm) long, are oval, tapered toward the base, have wavy toothed margins and are oppositely attached to a square prostrate stem that is swollen where leaves attach (nodes)

Bloom: year-round

Cycle/Origin: perennial; native

Habitat: disturbed sites, roadsides, pond margins, wet ditches

Range: throughout

Notes: Turkey Tangle Fogfruit is a short, mat-forming wildflower that spreads along the ground with prostrate stems. Tolerant of a variety of conditions, it can be found growing in dry rocky fields or along moist wetland margins. As a result, it adapts well to most gardens and is a superb alternative to more traditional ground covers. The small, matchstick-like flower clusters attract many insect pollinators, and the leaves serve as food for caterpillars of Phaon Crescent, Common Buckeye and White Peacock butterflies. Also known as Texas Fogfruit or Texas Frogfruit.

CLUSTER TYPE	FLOWER TYPE	LEAF TYPE	LEAF ATTACHMENT
Spike	Irregular	Simple	Opposite

fruit

TRAILING INDIGO
Indigofera spicata

Family: Pea or Bean (Fabaceae)

Height: 6-24" (15-61 cm)

Flower: slender spike cluster, ½-1½" (1-4 cm) long, of numerous small, pea-like pink flowers; cluster at the end of stalk; flowers open from the bottom of spike upward

Leaf: compound leaves made up of 5-7 oblong hairy leaflets; each leaflet, ½-1¼" (1-3 cm) long; leaves alternately attached to reclining, branched, green-to-bronze stem

Fruit: clusters of elongated green pods; each pod, ½-¾" (1-2 cm) long, is 4-sided, hairy and turns brown with age, splitting to release several small seeds

Bloom: year-round

Cycle/Origin: annual; non-native

Habitat: open disturbed sites, lawns, fields, pastures

Range: throughout Florida, except in the panhandle

Notes: Unlike Hairy Indigo (pg. 115), its larger shrubby relative, Trailing Indigo is a low-growing, mat-forming annual weed arising from a long vertical root (taproot). Spread by seed, it easily invades disturbed areas and cultivated landscapes such as lawns and open fields. This native plant of Africa and tropical Asia has naturalized throughout the Florida peninsula. It is the favorite host of caterpillars of the diminutive Ceraunus Blue butterfly.

CLUSTER TYPE	FLOWER TYPE	LEAF TYPE	LEAF ATTACHMENT	FRUIT
Spike	Irregular	Compound	Alternate	Pod

POWDERPUFF
Mimosa strigillosa

Family: Pea or Bean (Fabaceae)

Height: 6-9" (15-23 cm)

Flower: showy solitary round cluster, ¾-1¼" (2-3 cm) long, of many small tubular pink flowers; flower parts (stamens, including yellow anthers full of pollen) extend beyond tube, making flower cluster appear tipped in yellow; cluster on long upright stalk

Leaf: green-to-dark bluish green leaves, 2-6" (5-15 cm) long, are twice compound, divided into 4-8 pairs of oblong leaflets that are again divided into 10-15 pairs of tiny subleaflets

Fruit: hairy narrow oblong pod, 1-3" (2.5-7.5 cm) long, is green, turning brown and splitting to release seeds

Bloom: spring, summer, fall

Cycle/Origin: perennial; native

Habitat: moist to dry open habitats, disturbed sites

Range: northern and central Florida

Notes: Resembling small pompons, the flower heads are held high over the feathery foliage on long stalks. The ground-hugging stems can extend for several feet in all directions, overlapping to create a dense mat. Drought-tolerant, it quickly spreads in most any sunny location, but doesn't overtake neighboring vegetation. Like many *Mimosa* species, the tiny subleaflets are very sensitive to disturbance or touch—one can actually watch them move as they fold up or close.

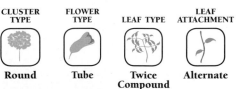

CLUSTER TYPE	FLOWER TYPE	LEAF TYPE	LEAF ATTACHMENT	FRUIT
Round	Tube	Twice Compound	Alternate	Pod

fruit

BEAUTYBERRY
Callicarpa americana

Family: Verbena (Verbenaceae)

Height: 4-8' (1.2-2.4 m)

Flower: dense round cluster, ¾-2" (2-5 cm) wide, of several small, 5-lobed, short-stalked, pink-to-pinkish white flowers; clusters in pairs in upper leaf attachments

Leaf: oval to elliptical, hairy leaves, 2½-6½" (6-16 cm) long, tapered at tips and bases, toothed edges, on short stalks, attached to ascending or spreading stem

Fruit: rounded clusters of tiny berry-like fruit encircling the stem; each round green fruit, ⅛" (.4 cm) wide, turns purple when ripe

Bloom: spring, summer

Cycle/Origin: perennial; native

Habitat: moist to slightly dry sites, open woodlands, forest margins, easements

Range: throughout

Notes: A common deciduous shrub widely used as a garden ornamental. The small flowers give way to very showy, rounded clusters of wine-colored, berry-like fruit equally spaced along the often spreading branches. In fact, *Callicarpa* is from two Greek words that together mean "beautiful fruit." An important food for wildlife, the fleshy fruits persist well into winter and are eaten by many bird, small mammal and deer species. American Indians used a root and leaf tea to treat rheumatism, fever, malaria and stomach ailments.

CLUSTER TYPE	FLOWER TYPE	LEAF TYPE	LEAF ATTACHMENT	FRUIT
Round	Regular	Simple	Opposite	Berry

fruit

LANTANA
Lantana camara

Family: Verbena (Verbenaceae)

Height: 2-6' (.6-1.8 m); shrub

Flower: bicolored flat cluster, 1-2" (2.5-5 cm) wide, of several small tubular flowers, each widely flaring at the mouth; flower color highly variable (may be pink, orange, yellow, lavender or cream); flowers change color with age

Leaf: oval to elliptical leaves, 1-5" (2.5-13 cm) long, are textured, rough and hairy with toothed margins; oppositely attached to multi-branched woody stem

Fruit: clusters of small berry-like fruit; each fruit, ¼" (.6 cm) wide, is green, turning blue to purple when ripe

Bloom: year-round

Cycle/Origin: perennial; non-native

Habitat: pinelands, dry woods, roadsides, disturbed sites, virtually any open areas

Range: throughout

Notes: This easy-to-grow, densely branched, woody shrub is often planted as an ornamental. A tough native of West Indies, it tolerates intense Florida heat and (once established) even drought. Despite its wide use, it is considered invasive. The flowers change color as they age (the youngest are in the center), resulting in a showy, two-toned cluster that attracts butterflies. Stems and leaves have stiff rough hairs and emit a distinct, somewhat unpleasant odor when rubbed.

CLUSTER TYPE	FLOWER TYPE	LEAF TYPE	LEAF ATTACHMENT	FRUIT
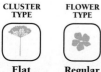				
Flat	Regular	Simple	Opposite	Berry

ROSY CAMPHORWEED
Pluchea baccharis

Family: Aster (Asteraceae)

Height: 12-36" (30-91 cm)

Flower: small fuzzy flat cluster, 1-2" (2.5-5 cm) wide, of numerous tubular pink disk flowers only (no ray flowers); clusters are at the ends of stems

Leaf: lance-shaped or oval, grayish green-to-silvery green leaves, 1½-4" (4-10 cm) long, are hairy with toothed margins; stalkless or clasping; alternately attached to an upright stem

Bloom: spring, summer, fall

Cycle/Origin: perennial; native

Habitat: moist pinelands, wet ditches, marshes, swamp margins

Range: throughout

Notes: The thick leaves of Rosy Camphorweed are very hairy and give the plant an attractive, overall gray-to-silver appearance that helps accentuate the fuzzy pink flower heads. The blooms attract numerous species of small butterflies and other pollinating insects. It is common in the wild throughout Florida, but very rarely seen in cultivation. Historically, the aromatic leaves were stuffed into bedding to help repel fleas, giving rise to another common name, Marsh Fleabane.

CLUSTER TYPE	FLOWER TYPE	LEAF TYPE	LEAF ATTACHMENT	LEAF ATTACHMENT
Flat	Composite	Simple	Alternate	Clasping

HENBIT DEAD-NETTLE
Lamium amplexicaule

Family: Mint (Lamiaceae)

Height: 6-15" (15-38 cm)

Flower: round cluster, 2-3" (5-7.5 cm) wide, of several 2-lipped elongated flowers; each flower, ½-1" (1-2.5 cm) long; hairy, dark pink upper lip; 2-lobed lower lip is pale pink with darker pink spots

Leaf: textured rounded leaves, ¾-1" (2-2.5 cm) wide, have 5 toothed lobes; upper leaves stalkless and attached below the flower clusters; lower leaves stalked; hairy ascending square stem

Bloom: winter, spring

Cycle/Origin: annual; non-native

Habitat: disturbed areas, old fields, roadsides, lawns

Range: northern and central Florida

Notes: Introduced from Eurasia and northern Africa, this colorful wildflower has naturalized throughout North America and is regarded as a minor weed of croplands, lawns and other open landscapes. A cool-season annual in Florida, blooming during the winter and early spring. Henbit Dead-nettle is tolerant of a wide range of growing conditions and often forms dense colonies that can cover large areas. It is entirely edible raw. Although a member of the Mint family, the plant's young shoots and leaves have a sweet, grassy flavor and are tasty in salads.

CLUSTER TYPE	FLOWER TYPE	LEAF TYPE	LEAF ATTACHMENT
Round	**Irregular**	**Simple Lobed**	**Opposite**

COASTAL PLAIN CHAFFHEAD
Carphephorus corymbosus

Family: Aster (Asteraceae)

Height: 12-36" (30-91 cm)

Flower: large flat cluster, 2-4" (5-10 cm) wide, composed of many flower heads, each with many tubular, bright pink disk flowers (no ray flowers); clusters atop a single stem

Leaf: elliptical basal leaves, 2½-8" (6-20 cm) long, with smooth edges; stem leaves are alternate and smaller

Bloom: summer, fall

Cycle/Origin: perennial; native

Habitat: dry soils, pinelands, open forests, disturbed sites

Range: peninsular Florida

Notes: Also called Florida Paintbrush for the individual fuzzy flower heads that resemble a painter's brush. The flat-topped clusters of these flower heads are called corymbs. In fact, the species name *corymbosus* means "full of corymbs," referring to the flower clusters. The pink clusters are atop a tall leafy stem and attract many types of butterflies and other insects. Of the five species of *Carphephorus* found in Florida, Coastal Plain Chaffhead is the only one mostly found in dry upland habitats.

CLUSTER TYPE	FLOWER TYPE	LEAF TYPE	LEAF ATTACHMENT	LEAF ATTACHMENT
Flat	Composite	Simple	Alternate	Basal

PINEWOODS MILKWEED
Asclepias humistrata

Family: Milkweed (Asclepiadaceae)

Height: 8-28" (20-71 cm)

Flower: loose round cluster, 2½-3½" (6-9 cm) wide, of many pale, ashy pink flowers; each flower, ¼" (.6 cm) wide, with 5 downward-curving petals and a deeply divided crown, made up of 5 scoop-shaped "hoods" and 5 inward-curving, beak-like "horns"

Leaf: broad oval leaves, 2-4" (5-10 cm) long, pale green to purple with pale pink veins; sprawling or rising pink stem

Fruit: elongated curved green pod, 3-5" (7.5-13 cm) long, tapering toward the tip; turns brown; splits open to release many dark brown seeds, each with cottony plumed tufts that carry it away on the wind

Bloom: spring, summer

Cycle/Origin: perennial; native

Habitat: sandy disturbed sites, sandhills, dry pinelands

Range: throughout

Notes: Frequently occurs in dry sandy pinelands. Monarch butterflies on their flight northward in spring lay their eggs on the foliage, which becomes an important food for the resulting caterpillars. Its flower clusters are visited by a wide variety of other nectar-seeking butterflies such as swallowtails, hairstreaks and skippers. *Humistrata* means "ground spreading," for its low, sprawling growth habit.

CLUSTER TYPE	FLOWER TYPE	LEAF TYPE	LEAF ATTACHMENT	LEAF ATTACHMENT	FRUIT
Round	Irregular	Simple	Opposite	Clasping	Pod

DOWNY PHLOX
Phlox pilosa

Family: Phlox (Polemoniaceae)

Height: 12-24" (30-61 cm)

Flower: loose flat cluster, 2-4½" (5-11 cm) wide, composed of few to several pink-to-lavender flowers; each flower, 1" (2.5 cm) wide, with 5 spatula-shaped petals fused at their bases to form a narrow tube

Leaf: hairy narrow lance-shaped leaves, 1-3" (2.5-7.5 cm) long, are stalkless; oppositely attached to a hairy, slender, upright to sprawling stem

Bloom: spring, summer

Cycle/Origin: perennial; native

Habitat: dry open woodlands, thickets, bluffs

Range: northern and central Florida

Notes: This delightful wildflower is one of seven *Phlox* species found in Florida. "Downy" in the common name and the species name *pilosa*, meaning "hairy," refer to the slender stems and leaves covered in soft hairs that give them an overall downy feel. The showy flowers are slightly fragrant and attract a variety of insect pollinators from bumblebees to butterflies. About nine varieties of this species occur throughout eastern half of the United States. American Indians used a tea made from the leaves as a wash to help treat eczema.

CLUSTER TYPE

Flat

FLOWER TYPE

Regular

LEAF TYPE

Simple

LEAF ATTACHMENT

Opposite

ANNUAL PHLOX
Phlox drummondii

Family: Phlox (Polemoniaceae)

Height: 8-24" (20-61 cm)

Flower: flat cluster, 3-5" (7.5-13 cm) wide, of several star-shaped flowers; flower color is variable (dark pink, lavender or red, often with white or darker contrasting center; can even be all white); each flower has 5 broad petals fused at their bases to form a narrow tube; clusters at ends of flower stalks (terminal)

Leaf: hairy lance-shaped leaves, 1½-4" (4-10 cm) long; upper leaves alternate, lower leaves are opposite; attached to a hairy sticky upright stem

Bloom: winter, spring, summer

Cycle/Origin: annual; non-native

Habitat: dry sandy open sites, disturbed areas, roadsides, fields

Range: throughout

Notes: Native to Texas, Annual Phlox has escaped cultivation and naturalized widely throughout the Southeast. An extremely showy, conspicuous, early-season wildflower that often grows in masses, forming expanses in open meadows and along roadways throughout Florida. Flowers are fragrant and extremely variable in color, ranging from all white to shades of pink and lavender (see inset) to maroon. The species name *drummondii* is for Thomas Drummond, who first described the species.

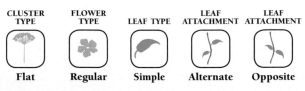

CLUSTER TYPE	FLOWER TYPE	LEAF TYPE	LEAF ATTACHMENT	LEAF ATTACHMENT
Flat	Regular	Simple	Alternate	Opposite

fruit

ROUGE PLANT
Rivina humilis

Family: Pokeweed (Phytolaccaceae)

Height: 1-5' (30-152 cm)

Flower: upright spike cluster, 3-6" (7.5-15 cm) long, of many tiny pale pink-to-pinkish white flowers, each less than ⅛" (.4 cm) wide, with 4 petal-like sepals

Leaf: oval to lance-shaped, dark green leaves, 1-6" (2.5-15 cm) long, are shiny with smooth wavy edges, broader at the bases and taper toward the tips; alternately attached with short leafstalks to upright stem

Fruit: small green berry, ¼" (.6 cm) wide, turning bright red when ripe

Bloom: year-round

Cycle/Origin: perennial; native

Habitat: disturbed areas, forests, coastal sites

Range: central and southern Florida

Notes: This attractive, shrub-like plant provides a splash of color to sun-dappled sites. The pale pink flowers and the berries are often present at the same time. Rouge Plant's ripe berries are glossy, nearly translucent bright red and have been used by American Indians as a source for dye. Also called Bloodberry. Although toxic to humans, the berries are a favorite food of many species of birds. The leaves were used to help treat wounds and contain properties that slow the growth of bacteria. Salt tolerant, Rouge Plant is a useful addition to any coastal landscape.

CLUSTER TYPE	FLOWER TYPE	LEAF TYPE	LEAF ATTACHMENT	FRUIT
Spike	Regular	Simple	Alternate	Berry

BAYBEAN
Canavalia rosea

Family: Pea or Bean (Fabaceae)

Height: 10-20' (3-6.1 m); vine

Flower: spike cluster, 3-8" (7.5-20 cm) long, with several large, pea-like, purplish pink flowers; each flower, 1½-2" (4-5 cm) long, with 2 lips and a white throat; clusters are at the ends of long stalks

Leaf: bright green compound leaves divided into 3 oval leaflets; each leaflet, 2-3" (5-7.5 cm) long; leaves alternately attached to a spreading branched stem

Fruit: elongated, slightly curved pod, 1½-3½" (4-9 cm) long, with a pointed tip; green, turning brown at maturity

Bloom: year-round

Cycle/Origin: perennial; native

Habitat: beaches, dunes, coastal sites

Range: central and southern Florida

Notes: This Pea or Bean family member is a low-growing vine of coastal lands and beaches. Its fleshy trailing stems can extend for many feet and form intertwined mats of vegetation that help stabilize dunes from erosion. Grows rapidly and makes an excellent ground cover. Also great for xeriscaping (a type of drought-tolerant landscaping), as the large thick leaflets often fold up during the heat of the day. The seeds are edible, but must be cooked or roasted before being consumed.

CLUSTER TYPE	FLOWER TYPE	LEAF TYPE	LEAF ATTACHMENT	FRUIT
	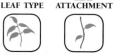	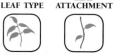		
Spike	Irregular	Compound	Alternate	Pod

fruit

HAIRY INDIGO
Indigo hirsuta

Family: Pea or Bean (Fabaceae)

Height: 2-5' (61-152 cm)

Flower: many small, pea-like, reddish pink flowers in a large slender spike cluster, 3-8" (7.5-20 cm) long; cluster at the end of stalk; flowers at the bottom of the spike open first

Leaf: 5-9 hairy oblong leaflets, each ¾-1½" (2-4 cm) long, make up the compound leaves, which are alternately attached to a hairy branched stem that is green to bronze

Fruit: clusters of hairy pods; each 4-sided green pod, ¾-1" (2-2.5 cm) long, is elongated, turns brown, splits at maturity and releases several small seeds

Bloom: summer, fall

Cycle/Origin: annual; non-native

Habitat: open disturbed sites

Range: throughout

Notes: Hairy Indigo is a robust, shrub-like annual that easily spreads by seed and is well adapted to low-nutrient soils, colonizing disturbed areas. Introduced from Africa and Southeast Asia, it has naturalized throughout the southeastern United States, where it is considered a nuisance weed. The species name *hirsuta* is derived from the Latin word for "hairy." In fact, the leaves, stems and seedpods of the plant are all noticeably hairy.

CLUSTER TYPE	FLOWER TYPE	LEAF TYPE	LEAF ATTACHMENT	FRUIT
Spike	Irregular	Compound	Alternate	Pod

SHOWY MILKWORT
Polygala violacea

Family: Milkwort (Polygalaceae)

Height: 6-20" (15-50 cm)

Flower: loose short spike cluster, 3-9" (7.5-23 cm) long, composed of small pink flowers, each with yellow-tipped petals and 2 oval petal-like sepals on each side, resembling ears

Leaf: uniformly narrow to lance-shaped leaves, ¾-2" (2-5 cm) long, with smooth edges; alternately attached to a thin upright stem

Bloom: spring, summer, fall

Cycle/Origin: perennial; native

Habitat: pinelands, roadsides, fields, open sites

Range: throughout

Notes: The flowers of this delicate wildflower are reminiscent of a small orchid. It is one of about 23 species of milkwort found in Florida, most of which occur in quite compact, but very distinctive clusters, and have irregular flowers. The genus name *Polygala* means "much milk" and refers to the plant's herbal properties, which are purported to improve lactation in nursing mothers. *Violacea*, the species name of Showy Milkwort, has been changed from *grandiflora*.

CLUSTER TYPE	FLOWER TYPE	LEAF TYPE	LEAF ATTACHMENT
Spike	Irregular	Simple	Alternate

SWEET PINXTER AZALEA
Rhododendron canescens

Family: Heath (Ericaceae)

Height: 3-12' (.9-3.7 m); shrub

Flower: dense round cluster, 4-8" (10-20 cm) wide, of several pink-to-whitish pink flowers, 2-3" (5-7.5 cm) long; flower has 5 wavy petals fused at their bases, forming a tube and broadly flaring at the mouth; very long, upward-curving flower parts (pistil and stamens) protrude from tube well beyond the petals

Leaf: hairy elliptical leaves, 1½-3½" (4-9 cm) long, alternately attached to an upright multi-branched stem

Fruit: cylindrical, hairy, reddish brown capsule, ½-¾" (1-2 cm) long, splits open in late summer to release seeds

Bloom: early spring

Cycle/Origin: perennial; native

Habitat: moist acidic soils, woodlands with partial shade, stream banks, swamp margins

Range: northern Florida

Notes: Sweet Pinxter Azalea, along with Orange Azalea (pg. 61), are among five *Rhododendron* species found in Florida and are arguably the most well known. The showy, abundant and fragrant blooms burst open in early spring (starting before the leaves fully emerge), making it a widely popular ornamental for home landscapes. Species name *canescens* means "to become white or gray" and refers to the pale hairs on the deciduous leaves and the branches.

CLUSTER TYPE	FLOWER TYPE	LEAF TYPE	LEAF ATTACHMENT	FRUIT
Round	Regular	Simple	Alternate	Pod

FLORIDA HEDGE-NETTLE
Stachys floridana

Family: Mint (Lamiaceae)

Height: 8-18" (20-45 cm)

Flower: spike cluster, 4-9" (10-23 cm) long, of whorls of pale pink flowers encircling the stem and spaced along the stem's upper portion; each flower, ¼-½" (.6-1 cm) long, has an upper hood-like lip and a 3-lobed lower lip that is dotted with purple

Leaf: lance-shaped leaves, ¾-3" (2-7.5 cm) long, with scalloped edges; oppositely attached with short leafstalks to an upright square stem

Bloom: year-round

Cycle/Origin: annual; native

Habitat: wet woodlands, disturbed sites, yards, lawns

Range: throughout

Notes: This attractive Mint family member is an aggressive wildflower that spreads rapidly and can quickly overtake moist sites. As a result, it is an often hard-to-control weed of yards, gardens and turfgrass. Also called Rattlesnake Weed, it has underground white tubers (rhizomes) that are swollen and segmented, resembling the tail of a rattlesnake. The rhizomes are edible. Genus name *Stachys* is derived from a Greek word for "spike" and refers to the shape of the flower cluster.

CLUSTER TYPE	FLOWER TYPE	LEAF TYPE	LEAF ATTACHMENT
Spike	**Irregular**	**Simple**	**Opposite**

LADY LUPINE
Lupinus villosus

Family: Pea or Bean (Fabaceae)

Height: 10-24" (25-61 cm)

Flower: large spike cluster, 5-10" (13-25 cm) long, of numerous pea-shaped, pink-to-lavender flowers; uppermost petal (standard) has a prominent, dark reddish purple spot

Leaf: hairy, silvery green leaves, 3-6" (7.5-15 cm) long, are elliptical, long-stalked and alternate on an upright or reclining, often branched, hairy stem

Fruit: curved bean-like pod, 1½-2" (4-5 cm) long, with a pointed tip and densely covered with long shaggy silvery hairs

Bloom: spring

Cycle/Origin: perennial; native

Habitat: disturbed sites, pinelands, dry woods, pastures

Range: northern and central Florida

Notes: It is hard to imagine a lovelier wildflower when in bloom than Lady Lupine. The statuesque pink flower spikes, often many per plant, tower above the downy, silvery green foliage and provide a very colorful display. In fact, all parts of the plant are densely covered with noticeable silvery hairs. Well adapted to dry sandy habitats, the robust plants arise from a woody main root (taproot) and often have several reclining or ascending branched stems. Each plant may reach several feet in diameter.

CLUSTER TYPE	FLOWER TYPE	LEAF TYPE	LEAF ATTACHMENT	FRUIT
Spike	**Irregular**	**Simple**	**Alternate**	**Pod**

SOUTHERN BEEBLOSSOM
Gaura angustifolia

Family: Evening-primrose (Onagraceae)

Height: 2-6' (.6-1.8 m)

Flower: loose branched spike cluster, 2-15" (5-38 cm) long, of flowers (white in the evening, turning pink by morning), each with 4 spatula-shaped petals, 8 broadly spreading flower parts (stamens) and backed by 4 narrow downward-pointing sepals

Leaf: lance-shaped, grayish green-to-green leaves, 1-5" (2.5-13 cm) long, stalkless with toothed or smooth edges; alternately attached to a slender upright stem

Fruit: 4-sided brown capsule, ½" (1 cm) long

Bloom: spring, summer, fall

Cycle/Origin: perennial; native

Habitat: disturbed areas, roadsides, dry woods, pinelands, coastal sites

Range: throughout

Notes: A slender plant with tall arching stems and branched airy flower spikes. Like other members in the *Gaura* genus, this is a somewhat weedy plant of dry sandy soils across the southern U.S. Aptly named "Beeblossom," the blooms are often visited by bees and other insects. Also called Morning Honeysuckle, the delicate, spider-like white flowers open in the evening and turn pink by early the next day before quickly wilting with the heat of the sun. Several cultivated species of beeblossom are sold as garden ornamentals.

CLUSTER TYPE	FLOWER TYPE	LEAF TYPE	LEAF ATTACHMENT	FRUIT
Spike	Irregular	Simple	Alternate	Pod

SHORTLEAF BLAZING STAR
Liatris tenuifolia

Family: Aster (Asteraceae)

Height: 2-6' (.6-1.8 m)

Flower: slender, elongated, dense spike cluster, 8-15" (20-38 cm) long, of numerous shaggy, tubular, 5-lobed disk flowers, each ¼-½" (.6-1 cm) long; each flower head lacks ray flowers and is on a short flower stalk; cluster on long upright stalk

Leaf: uniformly thin leaves, 3-12" (7.5-30 cm) long; alternately attached to an upright stem; leaves near the base of plant are much longer than those higher up the stem; uppermost leaves are very narrow and pressed up close (nearly parallel) to the stem

Bloom: summer, fall

Cycle/Origin: perennial; native

Habitat: sandy soils, pinelands, dry woods

Range: throughout

Notes: A handsome, late-season bloomer of pinelands and dry open woodlands. The species is aptly named *tenuifolia*, meaning "thin slender leaves." Its leaves are extremely narrow and closely resemble pine needles. The densely clumped plants resemble tufts of grass until they begin to bloom, when they send up tall and slender wand-like flower stalks. The small fuzzy flower heads are irresistibly attractive to butterflies, offering a wealth of nectar, but tend to be not as showy as those of other species of blazing star.

CLUSTER TYPE	FLOWER TYPE	LEAF TYPE	LEAF ATTACHMENT

Spike	Composite	Simple	Alternate

TRUMPETWEED
Eupatoriadelphus fistulosus

Family: Aster (Asteraceae)

Height: 6-10' (1.8-3 m)

Flower: large round cluster, 7-18" (18-45 cm) wide, of hundreds of fuzzy, dull mauve-to-pink flower heads on multiple flower stalks; each flower head is composed of several disk flowers only, lacking ray flowers

Leaf: downward-arching, lance-shaped, dark green leaves, 3½-12" (9-30 cm) long, with toothed margins; leaves are on long leafstalks and attached in whorls of 4-7 around a stout, upright and hollow, purplish green stem

Bloom: summer, fall

Cycle/Origin: perennial; native

Habitat: roadsides, moist open woodlands, forest edges, wet meadows, marshes

Range: northern and central Florida

Notes: It is hard to imagine a more statuesque and impressive wildflower than Trumpetweed. Towering above the shoulders of most adults, the massive fuzzy flower clusters are a magnet for bees, butterflies and other pollinating insects. Also called Hollow Joe-pye Weed due to its hollow, straw-like stem. Performing well in wild or formal landscapes, it is a showy addition to the back border of any garden. Some botanists consider this species as a member of the genus *Eupatorium*.

CLUSTER TYPE	FLOWER TYPE	LEAF TYPE	LEAF ATTACHMENT
Round	**Composite**	**Simple**	**Whorl**

ELLIOTT ASTER
Symphyotrichum elliottii

Family: Aster (Asteraceae)

Height: 3-6' (.9-1.8 m)

Flower: small daisy-like flower head, ¼-½" (.6-1 cm) wide, composed of 20-50 elongated, lavender-to-purple petals (ray flowers) surrounding a reddish yellow center (disk flowers)

Leaf: lance-shaped leaves, 1-8" (2.5-20 cm) long, with toothed or smooth margins; leaves on lower part of plant are longer and wider than those on upper branches; leaves alternately attached to a smooth upright multi-branched stem

Bloom: summer, fall, winter

Cycle/Origin: perennial; native

Habitat: swamps, wet roadsides, ditches, wetland margins

Range: throughout

Notes: Elliott Aster is a showy, late-season wildflower that often continues to bloom well into early winter. The robust and leafy plants produce a mass of violet-colored flowers in the upper branches. Blooms offer an abundant source of nectar for bees, butterflies and other insects at a time when the floral resources are often sparse. The plant is a vigorous grower and spreads by underground stems (rhizomes) to form dense patches. Although it prefers moist soils, Elliott Aster is easily grown in the home garden if regularly watered.

FLOWER TYPE	LEAF TYPE	LEAF ATTACHMENT
Composite	**Simple**	**Alternate**

CLASPING VENUS'S LOOKING GLASS
Triodanis perfoliata

Family: Bellflower (Campanulaceae)

Height: 8-18" (20-45 cm)

Flower: star-shaped, bluish purple flower, ⅓-½" (.8-1 cm) wide, with 5 oblong pointed petals around a pale center; flowers occur in leaf attachments; upper flowers open, lower flower remain closed

Leaf: variable, but usually rounded heart-shaped leaves, ¼-1" (.6-2.5 cm) long, with toothed margins and alternately attached to and clasping an upright stem

Fruit: hairy, cylindrical, reddish brown capsule, ½-¾" (1-2 cm) long, splitting open to release shiny seeds

Bloom: winter, spring, summer

Cycle/Origin: annual; native

Habitat: disturbed sites, fields, landscaped areas

Range: northern and central Florida

Notes: Although considered a weed, this lovely wildflower is worth a closer look. The rounded leaves that appear to nearly encircle the stem, combined with the small but showy, purple-to-bright blue flowers, quickly differentiate it from virtually any other plant. Its unusual common name refers to the hand-held vanity mirror used by Venus, the Roman goddess of love, to admire her beauty. "Looking Glass" is also partly due to the plant's former genus, *Specularia*, which means "of mirrors" and refers to the shiny seeds. The upper flowers are visited by a variety of small insect pollinators.

FLOWER TYPE	LEAF TYPE	LEAF ATTACHMENT	LEAF ATTACHMENT	FRUIT
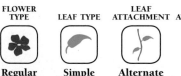				
Regular	Simple	Alternate	Clasping	Pod

OBLONGLEAF TWINFLOWER
Dyschoriste oblongifolia

Family: Acanthus (Acanthaceae)

Height: 6-18" (15-45 cm)

Flower: large funnel-shaped flower, ¾-1¼" (2-3 cm) long, with 5 purple-to-bluish lavender petals fused at their bases and broadly flaring at the mouth; darker purple spots or streaks in the throat; flowers borne in pairs from upper leaf attachment (axis)

Leaf: oval to oblong, dark green leaves, ¾-1½" (2-4 cm) long, are stalkless; oppositely attached to a narrow upright hairy stem

Bloom: spring, summer, fall

Cycle/Origin: perennial; native

Habitat: pinelands, dry woods

Range: throughout

Notes: The bright lavender flowers occur in pairs from the upper leaf attachments, thus "Twinflower" in the common name. This is a common, low-growing perennial of dry, partially shaded pinelands. Spreading by underground stems (rhizomes) or self-sown seed, the plants often form extensive dense colonies. A small, but highly ornamental species that makes a handsome ground cover, it is rapidly growing in popularity with native plant enthusiasts and growers. Oblongleaf Twinflower is one of several Florida host plants for Common Buckeye butterfly caterpillars.

FLOWER TYPE

Tube

LEAF TYPE

Simple

LEAF ATTACHMENT

Opposite

SPURRED BUTTERFLY PEA
Centrosema virginianum

Family: Pea or Bean (Fabaceae)

Height: 2-5' (61-152 cm); vine

Flower: showy lavender flower, ¾-1½" (2-4 cm) wide, with 5 petals; larger petal (standard) is broad, flattened and has a white center; other petals are smaller and form a distinct central spur; up to 3 flowers loosely arranged, occurring from leaf attachment

Leaf: compound leaves, divided into 3 oval or lance-shaped leaflets, each 1-3" (2.5-7.5 cm) long; leaves attached by long stalks to hairy twining stems

Fruit: flattened beaked green pod, 3-5½" (7.5-14 cm) long, turns brown; splits in half; halves curl up, remaining on vine; pods and blooms may be present together

Bloom: spring, summer, fall

Cycle/Origin: perennial; native

Habitat: dry open woodlands, forest margins, old fields

Range: throughout

Notes: Although structurally similar to other pea flowers, those of Spurred Butterfly Pea hang upside down, with the large and flattened standard petal facing downward. Genus name *Centrosema* is from the Greek words for "standard" and "spur," referring to the blunt spur on the back side of the standard petal near its base. A weak climber, the spindly vines twine loosely over low vegetation or across the ground. Host plant for Long-tailed Skipper butterfly caterpillars.

FLOWER TYPE	LEAF TYPE	LEAF ATTACHMENT	FRUIT
Irregular	Compound	Alternate	Pod

immature
seed heads

mature
seed heads

NETLEAF LEATHERFLOWER
Clematis reticulata

Family: Buttercup (Ranunculaceae)

Height: 3-12' (.9-3.7 m); vine

Flower: large solitary urn-shaped flower, 1-1½" (2.5-4 cm) long, lacks petals, but has 4 pale purple-to-violet, petal-like sepals; flower is fragrant and nods from a long slender stalk

Leaf: compound leaves of 3-9 leathery, elliptical to oval, widely spaced leaflets, each ½-3½" (1-9 cm) long, with raised veins; small tendril-like terminal leaflet; leaves opposite on sprawling or ascending stem

Bloom: spring, summer

Cycle/Origin: perennial; native

Habitat: pinelands, woodlands, forest margins

Range: northern and central Florida

Notes: Named for its leathery leaves with net-like raised veins. In fact, the species name *reticulata* means "network" in Latin, referring to the prominent pattern of the veins. Slender branches sprawl along the ground or climb on vegetation and have showy hanging flowers. As attractive as the blooms are, the spectacular seed heads provide the real show. Each pod in the seed head has a long and curving, feathery projection; seed heads stay on the plant for a long time.

FLOWER TYPE	LEAF TYPE	LEAF ATTACHMENT
Bell	Compound	Opposite

CAROLINA WILD PETUNIA
Ruellia caroliniensis

Family: Acanthus (Acanthaceae)

Height: 8-24" (20-61 cm)

Flower: small, funnel-like, lavender-to-purple (occasionally white) flower, 1-2" (2.5-5 cm) long, composed of 5 petals fused at their bases, forming a long tube and widely spreading at the mouth; flowers solitary or in small groups at leaf attachments at the end of stems (terminal)

Leaf: oval leaves, 1½-5" (4-13 cm) long, are oppositely attached with short stalks to a hairy upright stem

Fruit: small oval capsule, ½" (1 cm) long, is yellow, turning green, then brown with age; contains seeds

Bloom: spring, summer, fall

Cycle/Origin: perennial; native

Habitat: dry to moist soils, open woodlands, forest margins, disturbed sites

Range: throughout

Notes: Named because the showy flowers resemble those of the unrelated petunia, a common garden annual. Widespread throughout Florida, it tolerates a variety of growing conditions, and thus may be found in habitats ranging from sunny dry woodlands to shaded moist forests. Widely cultivated and has become a frequent addition to native gardens. The small seeds are forcibly expelled from the fruit capsule when mature and may travel some distance.

FLOWER TYPE	LEAF TYPE	LEAF ATTACHMENT	FRUIT
Tube	Simple	Opposite	Pod

143

PURPLE THISTLE
Cirsium horridulum

Family: Aster (Asteraceae)

Height: 1-5' (30-152 cm)

Flower: large round flower head, 1½-3" (4-7.5 cm) wide, atop a spiny base; flower color can be reddish purple, pink, yellow or white; 1 to several flower heads per plant

Leaf: strongly spiny, lance-shaped, grayish green leaves, 4-12" (10-30 cm) long, are deeply lobed, alternately attached and often downward-arching from a thick, hairy and seldom-branched stem; basal leaves are longest, forming a distinct rosette

Bloom: year-round

Cycle/Origin: perennial, biennial; native

Habitat: roadsides, old fields, pastures, open disturbed sites, pinelands, along freshwater or salt marshes

Range: throughout

Notes: The showy flower heads of this common wildflower range from deep reddish purple to pale yellow (thus another name, Yellow Thistle), or even powdery white (see inset). Like other thistles, this robust plant is dangerously spiny and often painful to brush against. May bloom periodically throughout the year, but peak blooms usually occur in spring or early summer. The flower heads attract insect pollinators such as swallowtail butterflies and skippers. Little Metalmark butterfly caterpillars feed upon the bristly leaves.

FLOWER TYPE	LEAF TYPE	LEAF ATTACHMENT	LEAF ATTACHMENT	LEAF ATTACHMENT
Composite	**Simple Lobed**	**Alternate**	**Clasping**	**Basal**

145

fruit

PURPLE PASSIONFLOWER
Passiflora incarnata

Family: Passionflower (Passifloraceae)

Height: 6-15' (1.8-4.6 m); vine

Flower: intricate lavender flower, 2½-3¼" (6-8 cm) wide, with 5 elliptical petals alternating with 5 elliptical sepals below a whorl of thin, wavy, lavender and white filaments that surround a greenish white center bearing 8 large flower parts

Leaf: dark green leaves, 2¾-6" (7-15 cm) long, deeply 3-lobed with fine-toothed margins; stem climbs using twining tendrils from leaf attachments

Fruit: large smooth oval berry, 1½-3" (4-7.5 cm) long, is green, becoming yellow and edible when ripe

Bloom: spring, summer, fall

Cycle/Origin: perennial; native

Habitat: disturbed sites, roadsides, woodland margins

Range: throughout

Notes: Although a member of a mostly tropical group of vines, it can survive freezing temperatures. The fruit fall off the vine when ripe and make a loud popping noise when stepped on, thus the plant is also called Maypop. A rambling vine used as ground cover or to cover trellises, it is becoming more widely available for purchase. Host plant for the caterpillars of several butterfly species such as Gulf Fritillaries and the Zebra Longwing, the state butterfly of Florida.

FLOWER TYPE	LEAF TYPE	LEAF ATTACHMENT	FRUIT
Regular	Simple Lobed	Alternate	Berry

MILE-A-MINUTE VINE
Ipomoea cairica

Family: Morning Glory (Convolvulaceae)

Height: 3-6' (.9-1.8 m); vine

Flower: lavender-to-pale pink (rarely white) flower, 2½-3½" (6-9 cm) long and wide, with a darker-colored center; 5 petals fused to form a funnel shape; flowers solitary or often in groups of 2-3

Leaf: hand-shaped leaves, appearing to be palmate and made up of individual leaflets, but actually are deeply cut to near the base into 5-7 lobes; central lobe, 2½-3½" (6-9 cm) long and wide, is the longest; leaves alternately attached to a smooth stem

Fruit: round green capsule, turning brown at maturity

Bloom: year-round

Cycle/Origin: perennial; non-native

Habitat: disturbed sites, roadsides

Range: central and southern Florida; scattered areas in the northern part of the state

Notes: Although its exact origin is uncertain, this twining perennial vine has naturalized across the world's tropics. "Mile-a-minute" in the common name is a nod to the rapid growth habit of the plant as it creeps or sprawls over trellises or other vegetation. Despite its wide use as a garden ornamental, this morning glory is usually considered an invasive weed.

FLOWER TYPE	LEAF TYPE	LEAF ATTACHMENT	FRUIT
Tube	Simple Lobed	Alternate	Pod

149

BRAZILIAN VERVAIN
Verbena brasiliensis

Family: Verbena (Verbenaceae)

Height: 3-7' (.9-2.1 m)

Flower: compact slender spike cluster, ¼-1½" (.6-4 cm) long, of small lavender flowers with 5 petals; groups of spike clusters at ends of long leafless stalks

Leaf: rough lance-shaped leaves, 1¼-3½" (3-9 cm) long, are dark green above, paler green below and have toothed edges; leaves oppositely attached to square rigid stem that is upright and often multi-branched

Bloom: year-round

Cycle/Origin: annual, perennial; non-native

Habitat: dry disturbed sites, roadsides, forest margins, fallow agricultural lands, fields

Range: northern and central Florida

Notes: A native of South America, this weedy introduced wildflower has naturalized throughout much of the Southeast, where it is a common invader of open disturbed sites. Brazilian Vervain is an annual or short-lived perennial that spreads rapidly by seed. The tall, multi-stemmed clumps often form dense stands that displace native species. Despite this drawback, each plant provides an extensive floral nectar buffet that is very popular with bees, wasps, butterflies and other pollinating insects.

CLUSTER TYPE	FLOWER TYPE	LEAF TYPE	LEAF ATTACHMENT
Spike	**Regular**	**Simple**	**Opposite**

151

SOUTH AMERICAN MOCK VERVAIN
Glandularia pulchella

Family: Verbena (Verbenaceae)

Height: 4-12" (10-30 cm)

Flower: flat cluster, 1-1½" (2.5-4 cm) wide, composed of many small, purple-to-lavender-to-pink flowers; each flower has a white throat and 5 petals; petals are fused at their bases and notched at the tips

Leaf: dark green-to-bluish green leaves, ¾-2½" (2-6 cm) long, are hairy, deeply cut into short lacy needle-like lobes and oppositely attached to ascending or spreading stems

Bloom: year-round

Cycle/Origin: perennial; non-native

Habitat: roadsides, old fields, disturbed sites

Range: throughout

Notes: As the first part of the common name suggests, this wild-flower is native to tropical areas in South America. It has escaped cultivation and naturalized across much of the southern United States. A low-growing, sprawling perennial forming large mats that may exceed several feet in diameter. Also called Moss Verbena, it is exceptionally drought tolerant and able to survive in a variety of harsh disturbed areas. The colorful blooms are a frequent sight along roads and attract butterflies and hummingbird moths. Easily propagated by seed or cuttings.

CLUSTER TYPE	FLOWER TYPE	LEAF TYPE	LEAF ATTACHMENT
Flat	Regular	Simple Lobed	Opposite

TAMPA MOCK VERVAIN
Glandularia tampensis

Family: Verbena (Verbenaceae)

Height: 12-24" (30-61 cm)

Flower: pinkish purple flat cluster, 1-1½" (2.5-4 cm) wide, composed of many small flowers, each with a white throat and 5 petals that are notched at the tips; petals are fused at their bases

Leaf: lance-shaped leaves, 1½-3" (4-7.5 cm) long, are papery, have toothed margins and are oppositely attached to an ascending or a spreading stem

Bloom: year-round

Cycle/Origin: perennial; native

Habitat: coastal dunes, hammocks, disturbed sites

Range: central Florida

Notes: This attractive, sprawling, short-lived wildflower is unique (endemic) to Florida. Now found in the central part of Florida, but was once more wide ranging, losing a significant amount of habitat due to extensive coastal development. It is listed by the state of Florida as an endangered species. Despite its rarity in the wild, Tampa Mock Vervain is widely cultivated and has become a commonly available landscape plant. It is particularly popular for butterfly gardens, and its low-growing habit makes it an ideal ground cover.

CLUSTER TYPE	FLOWER TYPE	LEAF TYPE	LEAF ATTACHMENT
Flat	**Regular**	**Simple**	**Opposite**

BAHAMA NIGHTSHADE
Solanum bahamense

Family: Nightshade (Solanaceae)

Height: 2-6' (.6-1.8 m)

Flower: short spike cluster, 2-6" (5-15 cm) long, bearing several small, star-shaped flowers; each flower, ½" (1 cm) wide, with 5 narrow backward-pointing lavender petals around protruding, golden yellow flower parts (stamens)

Leaf: lance-shaped leaves, 1-4" (2.5-10 cm) long, with smooth edges; alternate on a branched upright stem

Fruit: round green berry, ½" (1 cm) wide, turns red when ripe; berries hang in short rows from green stalks

Bloom: year-round

Cycle/Origin: perennial; native

Habitat: coastal areas

Range: central and southern Florida

Notes: A common, somewhat weedy, small shrub of open coastal habitats. Native to the Bahamas, to southern Florida and to western portions of the Caribbean. Belongs to the large Nightshade family, noted for the poisonous nature of many of its species, as well as edible members such as the common garden tomato, potato and green pepper. Also called *Berenjena de playa* or Beach Eggplant. The shiny red fruits of Bahama Nightshade are not edible. However, poultices made from its berries have been used to treat skin sores, giving rise to another common name, Cankerberry.

CLUSTER TYPE	FLOWER TYPE	LEAF TYPE	LEAF ATTACHMENT	FRUIT
Spike	Regular	Simple	Alternate	Berry

LYRELEAF SAGE
Salvia lyrata

Family: Mint (Lamiaceae)

Height: 8-24" (20-61 cm)

Flower: elongated spike cluster, 3-8" (7.5-20 cm) long, composed of whorls of several pale purple-to-bluish pink flowers; each flower, ¾-1¼" (2-3 cm) long, with a 3-lobed upper petal (lip) and a longer 2-lobed lower lip

Leaf: elliptical basal leaves, 3-8" (7.5-20 cm) long, in a rosette, are broader toward outer ends, have several deep symmetrical lobes and have toothed margins; smooth or lobed stem leaves are fewer, smaller and oppositely attached to a hairy square stem

Fruit: 4 nutlets in an open cup-shaped brown pod

Bloom: spring, summer, fall

Cycle/Origin: perennial; native

Habitat: disturbed sites, roadsides, forest margins, fields

Range: throughout

Notes: A common and widespread plant that is often overlooked, especially when compared to Tropical Sage (pg. 185) and other showier members of the genus *Salvia*. The pale flowers are visited by butterflies and hummingbirds. "Lyreleaf" refers to the similarity of the shape of the leaves to the curved string instrument used by the ancient Greeks. Although garden worthy, it spreads rapidly by seed and can become weedy.

CLUSTER TYPE	FLOWER TYPE	LEAF TYPE	LEAF ATTACHMENT	LEAF ATTACHMENT	FRUIT
Spike	Irregular	Simple Lobed	Opposite	Basal	Pod

AMERICAN WISTERIA
Wisteria frutescens

Family: Pea or Bean (Fabaceae)

Height: 6-40' (1.8-12.2 m); vine

Flower: large drooping spike cluster, 4-9" (10-23 cm) long, of numerous pea-like, lilac-to-purplish blue flowers; each flower, ¾" (2 cm) wide; flowers are unscented and only appear on new growth

Leaf: dark green compound leaves divided into 9-15 oval to lance-shaped leaflets; each leaflet, ¾-2½" (2-6 cm) long; leaves alternately attached on long stalks to a twining woody stem

Fruit: smooth narrow bean-like pod, 2-5" (5-13 cm) long, is green, turning brown at maturity

Bloom: spring, summer

Cycle/Origin: perennial; native

Habitat: moist soils, wet forests, stream margins, swamps

Range: northern Florida, mostly limited to the panhandle

Notes: A woody, deciduous vine with showy, pendulous blossoms. Climbs by twining, and while often simply scrambling over shrubs, is quite capable of reaching heights over 40 feet (12.2 m) in trees. The only native wisteria in Florida. Much less aggressive than its non-native invasive Asian counterpart, Chinese Wisteria (*W. sinensis*) (not shown), which is more readily available for purchase. Both serve as hosts for caterpillars of two of Florida's most attractive skipper butterflies species, Long-tailed Skipper and Silver-spotted Skipper.

CLUSTER TYPE	FLOWER TYPE	LEAF TYPE	LEAF ATTACHMENT	FRUIT
Spike	**Irregular**	**Compound**	**Alternate**	**Pod**

TALL IRONWEED
Vernonia angustifolia

Family: Aster (Asteraceae)

Height: 2-4' (61-122 cm)

Flower: loose branched flat cluster, 4-10" (10-25 cm) wide, composed of small fuzzy purple flower heads borne on long flower stalks; each head with small tubular disk flowers only, lacking ray flowers

Leaf: very narrow, dark green leaves, 2-4" (5-10 cm) long, are rough with smooth edges; leaves are many and alternate, getting progressively smaller going up along the smooth stiff upright stem

Bloom: summer, fall

Cycle/Origin: perennial; native

Habitat: sandy soils, dry woodlands, pinelands, roadsides, fields

Range: northern and central Florida

Notes: Although called Tall Ironweed, this rigidly upright wildflower rarely grows taller than 4 feet (1.2 m). Easily distinguished by its uniformly thin leaves from Giant Ironweed (pg. 167), which has lance-shaped leaves and prefers moist habitats. In fact, Tall's species name *angustifolia* refers to the narrow leaves. A clump-forming perennial that is gaining popularity for use in butterfly gardens. The genus *Vernonia* is named for the English botanist William Vernon.

CLUSTER TYPE	FLOWER TYPE	LEAF TYPE	LEAF ATTACHMENT
Flat	Composite	Simple	Alternate

165

in seed

GIANT IRONWEED
Vernonia gigantea

Family: Aster (Asteraceae)

Height: 4-8' (1.2-2.4 m)

Flower: loose irregular flat cluster, 6-12" (15-30 cm) wide, made up of small fuzzy purple flower heads, each with 10-30 small tubular disk flowers (ray flowers are absent)

Leaf: lance-shaped, dark green leaves, 4-12" (10-30 cm) long, are rough with sharp-toothed margins and pointed tips; leaves are numerous and alternately attached to a smooth to slightly hairy, stiff, upright, green-to-purplish green stem

Bloom: summer, fall

Cycle/Origin: perennial; native

Habitat: moist open woods, forest margins, roadsides, fields

Range: northern and central Florida

Notes: As its common name suggests, Giant Ironweed is a tall, robust and somewhat weedy-looking wildflower. Spreads by underground roots (rhizomes) and rapidly forms extensive clumps. Easy to grow, it makes an attractive addition to any native garden (especially if planted at the back of the border), but it is obviously not a good fit for small landscapes. The purple flower heads of the open clusters attract many butterflies and provide a very showy display, particularly when the plants are growing in masses.

CLUSTER TYPE	FLOWER TYPE	LEAF TYPE	LEAF ATTACHMENT
Flat	**Composite**	**Simple**	**Alternate**

TEXAS VERVAIN
Verbena halei

Family: Verbena (Verbenaceae)

Height: 12-30" (30-76 cm)

Flower: loose thin spike cluster, 8-14" (20-36 cm) long, composed of many small, pale purple flowers, each with 5 petals that are fused at their bases to form a widely flared funnel; spike blooms from the bottom upward

Leaf: highly variable-shaped leaves, ¾-4" (2-10 cm) long; lower leaves much longer and often with deep, narrow, toothed lobes; upper leaves are simple with smooth or toothed edges; leaves oppositely attached to a multi-branched upright square stem

Bloom: spring, summer

Cycle/Origin: perennial; native

Habitat: disturbed sites, roadsides, fields, dry forest margins

Range: northern and central Florida

Notes: Despite "Texas" in its common name, this vervain is widely distributed across the southern United States from North Carolina to Arizona. Drought tolerant, it persists in dry sandy disturbed sites and is commonly seen along roads. A prolific bloomer from February nearly to June. This upright perennial can easily be overlooked because of its airy appearance and very small, pale flowers. The slender spikes of flowers attract butterflies and other insects.

CLUSTER TYPE	FLOWER TYPE	LEAF TYPE	LEAF TYPE	LEAF ATTACHMENT
Spike	Tube	Simple	Simple Lobed	Opposite

SCARLET CREEPER
Ipomoea hederifolia

Family: Morning Glory (Convolvulaceae)

Height: 3-10' (.9-3 m); vine

Flower: small, scarlet red flower, ¾" (2 cm) wide, with an orangish red center; 5 petals are fused together to form a slender tube and abruptly spread out at end; few to many flowers in a group at the end of a long flower stalk

Leaf: extremely variable-shaped leaves, 1-4" (2.5-10 cm) long, from heart-shaped and toothed to 3 (or more) lobes, stalked, alternately attached to a smooth stem

Fruit: round green capsule, turning brown at maturity

Bloom: summer, fall

Cycle/Origin: annual; non-native

Habitat: disturbed sites, roadsides, fencerows

Range: throughout

Notes: A colorful morning glory found throughout the world's tropics and a common invasive weed of open disturbed areas across much of Florida. Aptly named, the scarlet red flowers of this twining vine are extremely showy and attract hummingbirds, many butterflies and sphinx moths. The short-lived blossoms open early in the morning and wilt rapidly by the heat of midday. Scarlet Creeper is a prolific grower and quickly covers any nearby vegetation. Species name *hederifolia* refers to a leaf shape that resembles those of ivy.

FLOWER TYPE	LEAF TYPE	LEAF TYPE	LEAF ATTACHMENT	FRUIT
Tube	Simple	Simple Lobed	Alternate	Pod

171

FLORIDA TASSELFLOWER
Emilia fosbergii

Family: Aster (Asteraceae)

Height: 12-30" (30-76 cm)

Flower: small cylindrical flower head, ½-1" (1-2.5 cm) long, of numerous red-to-dark pink disk flowers (no ray flowers) held below by green bracts; loose groups of flower heads (often drooping) on long, slender, usually branching stalks

Leaf: lower leaves are broad, upper leaves are lance-shaped; leaves have toothed edges and clasp an upright stem

Bloom: year-round

Cycle/Origin: perennial; non-native

Habitat: dry sunny sites, disturbed areas, pinelands, forest margins, roadsides, fields

Range: throughout

Notes: This weed from the Old World has naturalized throughout Florida and several other southern states, and in the American tropics. Often showing up in nursery material, it continues to spread with the ornamental landscape trade. Aptly named, the elongated flower heads confined in green bracts closely resemble small dangling tassels similar to those one might find on ornate pillows or draperies. The red flower heads are often visited by a variety of small insects including butterflies.

FLOWER TYPE	LEAF TYPE	LEAF ATTACHMENT	LEAF ATTACHMENT
Composite	Simple	Alternate	Clasping

TRUMPET HONEYSUCKLE
Lonicera sempervirens

Family: Honeysuckle (Caprifoliaceae)

Height: 12-16' (3.7-4.9 m); vine

Flower: trumpet-shaped red flower, 1-2" (2.5-5 cm) long, with 5 petals fused to form a long tube; flowers borne in whorled groups at the ends of stems

Leaf: smooth, broadly oval, evergreen leaves, 1-3" (2.5-7.5 cm) long, oppositely attached along stems; the leaves just below the flowers are united at their bases and completely surround the stems

Fruit: round green berry, ¼" (.6 cm) wide, turning red when ripe

Bloom: spring, summer, fall

Cycle/Origin: perennial; native

Habitat: open woods, forest margins, shrubby areas

Range: northern and central Florida

Notes: Exceptionally ornamental, Trumpet Honeysuckle is a slender woody vine that is ideal for the home landscape. Very easy to grow and can be used as a ground cover or to cover a trellis or arbor. Unlike its non-native relatives, this plant is will not grow out of control. Also called Coral Honeysuckle, its bright coral-to-brilliant red tubular flowers are a favorite nectar source for hummingbirds, and the small round berries that follow are consumed by songbirds. The species name *sempervirens* is from Latin words combined to mean "always green," referring to the evergreen leaves.

FLOWER TYPE	LEAF TYPE	LEAF ATTACHMENT	LEAF ATTACHMENT	FRUIT
Tube	Simple	Opposite	Perfoliate	Berry

fruit

SCARLET ROSE MALLOW
Hibiscus coccineus

Family: Mallow (Malvaceae)

Height: 4-9' (1.2-2.7 m)

Flower: very large flower, 6-8" (15-20 cm) wide, of 5 oval, broadly spreading red petals tapering at bases and surrounding a column of red flower parts; 5 large pointed green sepals (calyx) behind the petals; flowers on long stalks from the upper leaf attachments

Leaf: hand-shaped leaves, 5-6" (13-15 cm) long, with 3-5 narrow pointed lance-shaped leaflets; leaves on long stalks and alternately attached to stout upright stem

Fruit: rounded green capsule, 1-2" (2.5-5 cm) wide, turns brown; 5-chambered, splits open to release seeds

Bloom: spring, summer, fall

Cycle/Origin: perennial; native

Habitat: swamps, wet ditches, marshes, pond margins

Range: throughout

Notes: Seeing the massive, bright red flowers of Scarlet Rose Mallow in full bloom is truly a photographic moment for the wildflower enthusiast and novice alike. Slender robust stems arising from mature plants tower above other wetland vegetation and have airy hand-like leaves that resemble those of hemp plants. Although also called Swamp Hibiscus, in part for its preference of moist conditions, this tough perennial is well suited for home gardens and makes quite a statement when used in the back of a border.

FLOWER TYPE	LEAF TYPE	LEAF ATTACHMENT	FRUIT
Regular	**Palmate**	**Alternate**	**Pod**

narrow leaves

PAINTEDLEAF
Euphorbia cyathophora

Family: Spurge (Euphorbiaceae)

Height: 8-36" (20-91 cm)

Flower: red bases of leaf-like green bracts appear to be the petals of the flower, but the true flowers are in a flat cluster, ¼-1" (.6-2.5 cm) wide, made up of several tiny green flowers, each less than ⅛" (.4 cm) wide, and lacking petals

Leaf: highly variable-shaped, from fiddle- to lance-shaped to uniformly thin, 1½-7" (4-18 cm) long; edges also variable, from slightly toothed to deeply lobed; mostly oppositely (some alternately) attached to an upright stem

Bloom: year-round

Cycle/Origin: annual, perennial; native

Habitat: roadsides, disturbed sites, forest margins, pinelands, open woods

Range: throughout

Notes: Related to the traditional yuletide flower. Also called Wild Poinsettia or Fire-on-the-mountain. "Paintedleaf" refers to the showy red and green tops (actually leaf-like bracts) that are just below the cluster of true flowers. Highly variable-shaped leaves, ranging from broad and lobed (resembling the shape of a violin) to narrow and grass-like (see inset). The form of the plant also varies from densely branched to open and spindly. All parts of the plant are poisonous.

CLUSTER TYPE	FLOWER TYPE	LEAF TYPE	LEAF TYPE	LEAF ATTACHMENT	LEAF ATTACHMENT

Flat	Irregular	Simple	Simple Lobed	Alternate	Opposite

181

WOODLAND PINKROOT
Spigelia marilandica

Family: Logania (Loganiaceae)

Height: 18-24" (45-61 cm)

Flower: curving spike cluster, 3-4" (7.5-10 cm) long, composed of several showy flowers along 1 side of spike; each flower 1-2" (2.5-5 cm) long, with 5 red petals fused to form a long tube that is yellow inside and flares widely at the mouth into a yellow star shape

Leaf: narrow to broadly lance-shaped, dark green leaves, 2-5" (5-13 cm) long, stalkless and with smooth edges; oppositely attached to upright smooth stem

Fruit: round green pod, ¼-⅓" (.6-.8 cm) wide, turning black and exploding at maturity to expel seeds

Bloom: spring, summer

Cycle/Origin: perennial; native

Habitat: rich moist woodlands, stream banks

Range: panhandle of Florida

Notes: This clump-forming perennial is one of the most distinctive and attractive wildflowers found in Florida. Limited to the panhandle, it grows in the semi-shaded confines of rich hardwood forests, woodlands with calcium or limestone soils and on bluffs. Widely available from native nurseries and makes an outstanding shade garden plant. Also called Indian Pink or Wormgrass, American Indians used a tea brewed from the plant's root to expel intestinal parasites. The tubular flowers are particularly popular with hummingbirds.

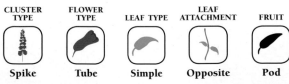

CLUSTER TYPE	FLOWER TYPE	LEAF TYPE	LEAF ATTACHMENT	FRUIT
Spike	Tube	Simple	Opposite	Pod

TROPICAL SAGE
Salvia coccinea

Family: Mint (Lamiaceae)

Height: 12-36" (30-91 cm)

Flower: elongated spike cluster, 3-8" (7.5-20 cm) long, composed of whorls of several red flowers; each flower, ¾-1¼" (2-3 cm) long, has a 2-lobed upper petal (lip) and a longer 3-lobed lower lip

Leaf: heart-shaped leaves, 1-3" (2.5-7.5 cm) long, are textured, have toothed margins and are oppositely attached with short stalks to an upright stem

Fruit: 4 nutlets in an elongated brown pod, ½" (1 cm) long

Bloom: year-round

Cycle/Origin: perennial; native

Habitat: disturbed sites, roadsides, forest margins, fields

Range: throughout

Notes: The showy, vibrant red flowers of Tropical Sage (also called Scarlet Sage) make it a popular choice for home gardens. Also a favorite since it is very easy to grow and cultivated forms in shades from white to pink are available for purchase. Tolerant of heat and drought, the plant performs well even under harsh Florida growing conditions. As a result, it is often used for naturalizing along roads and other easements. Although short-lived, it self-sows and can become weedy. The blooms are frequently visited by Cloudless Sulphur butterflies and by hummingbirds.

CLUSTER TYPE	FLOWER TYPE	LEAF TYPE	LEAF ATTACHMENT	FRUIT
Spike	Irregular	Simple	Opposite	Pod

fruit

CORALBEAN
Erythrina herbacea

Family: Pea or Bean (Fabaceae)

Height: 2-5' (61-152 cm); shrub

Flower: large showy spike cluster, 10-20" (25-50 cm) long, of tiered whorls of tubular, coral-to-scarlet red flowers, each 1-3" (2.5-7.5 cm) long; flowers protrude out at nearly right angles from the long flower stalk

Leaf: compound leaves, 4-8" (10-20 cm) long, with 3 distinct arrowhead-shaped leaflets; leaves alternately attached to a prickly stem

Fruit: long, dark brown-to-black pod, 3-7" (7.5-18 cm) long, constricted around the seeds, splits open at maturity to reveal many oval, bright red seeds

Bloom: winter, spring, summer

Cycle/Origin: perennial; native

Habitat: dry woods, thickets, pinelands, coastal dunes

Range: throughout

Notes: A striking shrub underutilized in landscaping. In frost-free areas, it sometimes reaches a height of 20 feet (6.1 m) or more. The prickly, widely spreading stems arising from the woody base die back to the ground in freezing weather. Showy red-orange blooms are a favorite of hummingbirds. Perhaps even more stunning are the long, sooty brown pods housing a chain-like line of extremely poisonous, shiny red seeds. Despite its strong narcotic and purgative properties, the plant has been used to treat many ailments.

CLUSTER TYPE	FLOWER TYPE	LEAF TYPE	LEAF ATTACHMENT	FRUIT
Spike	**Tube**	**Compound**	**Alternate**	**Pod**

CARDINALFLOWER
Lobelia cardinalis

Family: Bellflower (Campanulaceae)

Height: 2-4' (61-122 cm)

Flower: tall open spike, 12-24" (30-61 cm) long, of scarlet red flowers, 1½" (4 cm) wide, alternating on stem, with lower blooms opening before upper; each flower has 5 narrow petals (2 upper and 3 spreading lower) that unite to form a thin tube at its base

Leaf: toothed lance-shaped leaves, up to 6" (15 cm) long, nearly clasp the stem

Bloom: summer, fall

Cycle/Origin: perennial; native

Habitat: wet soils, shade, along streams and wetlands, swamps, moist woodlands

Range: northern Florida

Notes: Although limited in range, Cardinalflower is by far one of the most spectacular wildflowers of Florida. It is typically found growing in small patches along wetlands or in floodplain forests. This plant can be grown in gardens, but its roots need to be wet and its flowers must have some sunlight to effectively bloom. Cardinalflower is not very successful at reproducing, perhaps because it can be pollinated only by hummingbirds. Do not dig this plant from the wild–it can be purchased at garden centers. Its scarlet red flowers resemble the color of the bright red robes worn by Roman Catholic cardinals, thus its common name.

CLUSTER TYPE	FLOWER TYPE	LEAF TYPE	LEAF ATTACHMENT
Spike	Irregular	Simple	Alternate

COMMON CHICKWEED
Stellaria media

Family: Pink (Caryophyllaceae)

Height: 3-9" (7.5-23 cm)

Flower: star-shaped white flowers, ¼" (.6 cm)wide, found singly at the ends of tiny stalks; each of 5 petals is deeply divided, giving the appearance of 2 petals and making the flower look as though it actually has 10 petals

Leaf: toothless pointed-tipped leaves, ½-1" (1-2.5 cm) long, sit opposite one another on the stem; upper leaves clasp the stem; lower leaves attach by short thin leafstalks that are often covered in tiny hairs

Bloom: winter, spring

Cycle/Origin: annual; non-native

Habitat: wet or dry soils, disturbed sites, sun or shade

Range: northern and central Florida

Notes: A common, weak-stemmed plant that lays across the ground in large mats, displaying many flowers per plant. When its white flowers are open, they look like many tiny stars. Introduced from Europe, this invasive annual is an aggressive weed of disturbed sites, gardens and (occasionally) even lawns. Common Chickweed is a cool-season wildflower that typically blooms most prolifically in winter and early spring. The plant is edible.

FLOWER TYPE	LEAF TYPE	LEAF ATTACHMENT	LEAF ATTACHMENT
Regular	Simple	Opposite	Clasping

ROUNDLEAF BLUET
Houstonia procumbens

Family: Madder (Rubiaceae)

Height: ¼-1" (.6-2.5 cm)

Flower: upright, solitary, pure white flower, ¼" (.6 cm) wide, with a pale yellow throat and 4 (rarely 5) widely flaring, pointed petals that are fused at their bases

Leaf: small oval leaves, ⅓-½" (.8-1 cm) long, are somewhat fleshy and are oppositely attached to a short creeping stem

Bloom: winter, spring, summer

Cycle/Origin: perennial; native

Habitat: dry sandy areas, open woodlands, pinelands, disturbed sites

Range: throughout

Notes: Also called Innocence or Fairy Footprints, this diminutive and charming wildflower was previously in the genus *Hedyotis*. A low-growing perennial, the small plants form dense, nearly flat mats that can occasionally grow wider than 10 inches (25 cm). Species name *procumbens* refers to this prostrate growth habit. Roundleaf Bluet bursts into flower in late winter (when little else is in bloom), persisting through spring and flowering sporadically in summer.

FLOWER TYPE

Tube

LEAF TYPE

Simple

LEAF ATTACHMENT

Opposite

OAKLEAF FLEABANE
Erigeron quercifolius

Family: Aster (Asteraceae)

Height: 6-18" (15-45 cm)

Flower: small daisy-like flower head, ¼-½" (.6-1 cm) wide, composed of over 100 tiny white-to-lavender petals (ray flowers) surrounding a bright yellow center (disk flowers); each flower head sits atop a hairy flower stalk

Leaf: hairy, oval to lance-shaped, mostly basal leaves, ¾-4" (2-10 cm) long, are lobed or toothed, broadest at tips and tapering toward bases; stem leaves are few, smaller and alternately clasp a hairy stem

Bloom: winter, spring, summer

Cycle/Origin: annual; native

Habitat: open woodlands, forest margins, disturbed sites, roadsides

Range: throughout

Notes: One of eight species of *Erigeron* found in Florida, Oakleaf Fleabane is perhaps the most widespread and distinctive. The small, aster-like flower heads tower over the leaves on long, nearly leafless stalks, a characteristic that distinguishes them from asters. The species name *quercifolius* is derived from Latin and means "oak leaf," referring to the lobed, oak-like shape of the basal leaves. Dried fleabane plants were once stuffed into bedding to repel fleas and other pests.

FLOWER TYPE
Composite

LEAF TYPE
Simple

LEAF TYPE
Simple Lobed

LEAF ATTACHMENT
Alternate

LEAF ATTACHMENT
Clasping

LEAF ATTACHMENT
Basal

HERB-OF-GRACE
Bacopa monnieri

Family: Snapdragon (Scrophulariaceae)

Height: 3-10" (7.5-25 cm)

Flower: solitary funnel-shaped flower, ½" (1 cm) wide, composed of 5 white-to-pale bluish pink petals fused at their bases and broadly flaring at the mouth; flower occurs from leaf attachment (axis)

Leaf: thick and succulent oval leaves, ½-¾" (1-2 cm) long, are hairless, smooth-edged and stalkless; oppositely attached to a prostrate spreading stem

Bloom: year-round

Cycle/Origin: perennial; native

Habitat: moist soils, wet ditches along roads, edges of ponds and marshes, canal margins

Range: throughout

Notes: Also called Smooth Water Hyssop, this is a delicate, low-growing, aquatic or semiaquatic perennial of fresh and brackish water habitats. The broadly creeping stems of Herb-of-grace root where the leaves attach (nodes) and often form dense mats of vegetation. A reputed medicinal herb used in India. Reports indicate that plant extracts have shown significant promise to help enhance memory and motor function, as well as treat anxiety and depression. It is the host plant for White Peacock butterfly caterpillars.

FLOWER TYPE
Regular

LEAF TYPE
Simple

LEAF ATTACHMENT
Opposite

fruit

CAROLINA GERANIUM
Geranium carolinianum

Family: Geranium (Geraniaceae)

Height: 6-20" (15-50 cm)

Flower: pinkish white-to-light purple flower, ½" (1 cm) wide, of 5 notched oval petals and backed by hairy green bracts; lower flowers often with darker pink veins; flowers usually at ends of stems (terminal)

Leaf: overall round leaves, 1-3" (2.5-7.5 cm) wide, deeply divided into 5 lobes, each divided into more lobes with toothed edges; leaves alternate near the base of stem, opposite higher up and attach by long leaf-stalks to a slender, hairy, upright to sprawling stem

Fruit: tubular green capsule, ½-1" (1-2.5 cm) long, with long pointed tip; capsule turns brown and splits open to release small kidney-shaped seeds

Bloom: winter, spring, summer

Cycle/Origin: annual, biennial; native

Habitat: fields, roadsides, forest margins, open woods, sun

Range: throughout

Notes: This is a delicate spring wildflower with small but very attractive flowers. Weedy, it is an early invader of open disturbed sites, and it often forms large colonies. Also called Crane's Bill for the unusual "beaked" shape of the seed capsule, which resembles the head of a crane. The small seeds are eaten by a variety of songbirds and small mammals.

FLOWER TYPE	LEAF TYPE	LEAF ATTACHMENT	LEAF ATTACHMENT	FRUIT
Regular	Simple Lobed	Alternate	Opposite	Pod

SNOW SQUARESTEM
Melanthera nivea

Family: Aster (Asteraceae)

Height: 2-6' (.6-1.8 m)

Flower: small round button-like flower head, ½" (1 cm) wide, composed of tiny tubular white disk flowers only (lacking ray flowers) and black flower parts (anthers)

Leaf: rough, dark green leaves, ¾-2½" (2-6 cm) long, often 3-lobed and widest at their bases, with scalloped margins; opposite on a rigid, multi-branched, dark, square stem

Bloom: year-round

Cycle/Origin: perennial; native

Habitat: pinelands, open woods, disturbed sites, coastal areas

Range: throughout

Notes: Snow Squarestem is a bushy, densely branched plant tolerant of a variety of habitats, from sandy areas along the backshores of beaches and forested areas next to marshes to moist pinelands and open woodlands. Easily propagated from seed, it is an exceptional plant to use in pollinator and butterfly gardens. The genus name *Melanthera* is a combination of Greek words that translate to "black anthers," and the species name *nivea* refers to the snowy white color of the flower heads. This contrasting color combination also explains its other two (albeit lesser used) common names, Salt-and-pepper and Nonpareil (a chocolate drop covered with white sugar beads).

FLOWER TYPE	LEAF TYPE	LEAF ATTACHMENT
Composite	Simple Lobed	Opposite

RICE BUTTON ASTER
Symphyotrichum dumosum

Family: Aster (Asteraceae)

Height: 12-36" (30-91 cm)

Flower: small daisy-like flower head, ½-¾" (1-2 cm) wide, composed of many elongated white-to-lavender petals (ray flowers) surrounding a yellow center (disk flowers); flower heads borne in loose groups on arching flower stalks

Leaf: uniformly thin to narrowly lance-shaped leaves, 1-4" (2.5-10 cm) long, with smooth margins; leaves on lower part of plant are longer and wider than those on flowering branches; leaves alternately attached to a slender arching multi-branched stem

Bloom: summer, fall

Cycle/Origin: perennial; native

Habitat: pinelands, open woods, along roads, disturbed sites, fields

Range: throughout

Notes: This species is arguably the most common and widespread aster in Florida. It is extremely adaptable and can tolerate a variety of growing conditions, from moist to very dry. Also called Bushy Aster, the leafy stems are extensively branched, often resulting in a compact, shrubby plant. Rice Button Aster is adorned with a multitude of small flower heads in late summer and in autumn.

FLOWER TYPE	LEAF TYPE	LEAF ATTACHMENT
Composite	Simple	Alternate

205

fruit

TREAD SOFTLY
Cnidoscolus urens

Family: Spurge (Euphorbiaceae)

Height: 8-36" (20-91 cm)

Flower: small, pure white flower, ½-¾" (1-2 cm) wide, is star-shaped and has a center with divided flower parts; lacks petals, but has 5 elliptical petal-like sepals; flowers loosely clustered at end of stalk

Leaf: hairy, dark green leaves, 2½-6" (6-15 cm) long, with 3-5 lobes, toothed margins and pale veins; leaves resemble those of a maple tree; alternate on a hairy stem

Fruit: upright green capsule, ½-⅔" (1-1.6 cm) long; is round or oval, spiny, 3-segmented and splits open when mature to release 3 large seeds

Bloom: year-round

Cycle/Origin: perennial; native

Habitat: dry woodlands, roadsides, coastal areas

Range: throughout

Notes: Covered by short stinging hairs that release a caustic irritant, Tread Softly lives up to its name by delivering a painful burning sensation to any individual unlucky enough to brush against it. While the intense pain typically subsides after a few minutes, it can result in a skin rash that may last for days. Sensitive individuals may have more severe reactions. This unique perennial is common in dry sandy habitats and waste or disturbed sites.

FLOWER TYPE	LEAF TYPE	LEAF ATTACHMENT	FRUIT
Regular	Simple Lobed	Alternate	Pod

SOUTHERN DEWBERRY
Rubus trivialis

Family: Rose (Rosaceae)

Height: 3-10' (.9-3 m)

Flower: large, usually solitary flower, ¾-1½" (2-4 cm) wide, with 5 oblong white petals (often tinged with pink) around a center with many flower parts (stamens); flowers on short prickly flower stalks

Leaf: stiff, dark green, compound leaves, made up of 3-5 elliptical leaflets; each leaflet, ¾-2½" (2-6 cm) long, has coarse-toothed edges; leaves on spiny stalks; reclining bristly hairy stem; leaves often turn reddish green and persist on plant through the winter

Fruit: rounded berry-like red fruit, ½-1¼" (1-3 cm) long, turns black when ripe; looks similar to a blackberry

Bloom: winter, spring

Cycle/Origin: perennial; native

Habitat: dry woods, thickets, pinelands, roadsides

Range: throughout

Notes: Southern Dewberry is a trailing, vine-like, woody perennial with intertwining branches covered with red glandular hairs and short barbs. Blooms profusely early in the season. The ripe, plump, berry-like fruit that follows in late spring is edible raw and also is an important food resource for game birds, songbirds and a variety of small mammals. Species name *trivialis* means "commonplace," referring to its wide occurrence and overall abundance.

FLOWER TYPE	LEAF TYPE	LEAF ATTACHMENT	FRUIT
Regular	Compound	Alternate	Berry

fruit

Noyau Vine
Merremia dissecta

Family: Morning Glory (Convolvulaceae)

Height: 8-13' (2.4-4 m); vine

Flower: large white flower, 1¼-2¼" (3-5.5 cm) long and wide, with a red-to-purple center; 5 petals fused together to form a funnel shape

Leaf: hand-shaped leaves, 1½-4" (4-10 cm) long, appearing to be palmate and made up of individual leaflets, but actually are deeply cut to near the base into 7-9 lobes; stalked and alternately attached to a hairy stem

Fruit: green capsule, ½-¾" (1-2 cm) long, turning brown and splitting open at maturity

Bloom: spring, summer, fall

Cycle/Origin: perennial; non-native

Habitat: disturbed areas, forest margins, thickets

Range: throughout

Notes: First discovered in the Caribbean, Noyau Vine has been introduced to other tropical regions around the globe. Some say it may even be native to the southern U.S. "Noyau" is French for "kernel," referring to the nut of the bitter almond. The plant has an almond taste and scent, and has been used by many cultures as a condiment, medicine and an ornamental. An attractive climbing, twining vine that can grow longer than 13 feet (4 m). Despite its widespread garden use, it is considered a weedy pest in Florida.

FLOWER TYPE	LEAF TYPE	LEAF ATTACHMENT	FRUIT
Tube	Simple Lobed	Alternate	Pod

MAN-OF-THE-EARTH
Ipomoea pandurata

Family: Morning Glory (Convolvulaceae)

Height: 1-15' (.3-4.6 m); vine

Flower: large white flower, 2-6" (5-7.5 cm) wide and equally as long, has 5 petals fused together to form a funnel shape; center is purple to burgundy

Leaf: variable, mostly heart-shaped leaves, 2-6" (5-15 cm) long, with smooth margins and stalked; alternately attached to a smooth or sparsely short-haired stem

Fruit: round green capsule, turning brown at maturity; contains 4 dark seeds with long stiff hairs

Bloom: spring, summer, fall

Cycle/Origin: perennial; native

Habitat: dry to moist soils, disturbed areas, forest margins, riverbanks, open woodlands

Range: northern two-thirds of Florida

Notes: Also called Wild Potatovine due to its tuberous and starchy root, which is edible after being cooked and tastes similar to a cultivated sweet potato. The large underground root has been known to grow as long as 6 feet (1.8 m) and weigh as much as 15-30 pounds (6.8-13.5 kg), likely giving rise to the name Man-of-the-earth. The roots were collected by American Indians as a food source, and a tea brewed from the tuber was used medicinally as a diuretic or purgative, or an expectorant. The showy flowers typically open in the morning and are quite short-lived, wilting before day's end.

FLOWER TYPE	LEAF TYPE	LEAF ATTACHMENT	FRUIT
Tube	Simple	Alternate	Pod

SLIMLEAF PAWPAW
Asimina angustifolia

Family: Custard-apple (Annonaceae)

Height: 2-5' (61-152 cm)

Flower: large, creamy white-to-yellowish white flower, 2-3" (5-7.5 cm) wide, with 3 large outer petals, 3 smaller inner petals; flower parts (stamens) are packed together, forming a dense ball; petals often tinged with purple at the bases; flowers droop from new growth in the upper leaf attachments

Leaf: long, leathery, uniformly narrow to narrowly lance-shaped leaves, 2-8" (5-20 cm) long, are alternately attached to upright to spreading branches

Fruit: lopsided green berry, 1½-4" (4-10 cm) long, turning brown when ripe

Bloom: spring, summer

Cycle/Origin: perennial; native

Habitat: pinelands, open woods, fields, pastures, easements

Range: northern and central Florida

Notes: The showy flowers of Slimleaf Pawpaw are fragrant, but the crushed leaves emit a foul odor. Species name *angustifolia*, meaning "narrow leaves," aptly describes the shape of the foliage. The growth habit of gently arching branches spreading outward away from the base provide an overall rounded appearance to this common shrub. Slimleaf Pawpaw produces less abundant fruit than other pawpaw species. A host for caterpillars of Zebra Swallowtail butterflies.

FLOWER TYPE	LEAF TYPE	LEAF ATTACHMENT	FRUIT
Irregular	**Simple**	**Alternate**	**Berry**

WOOLLY PAWPAW
Asimina incana

Family: Custard-apple (Annonaceae)

Height: 2-4' (61-122 cm)

Flower: large, lemony-scented, creamy white flowers, 3-4" (7.5-10 cm) wide, with 3 large outer petals and 3 smaller inner petals; flower droops from the upper leaf attachment (axis)

Leaf: densely hairy, oval leaves, 2-4" (5-10 cm) long, are alternately attached to upright multi-branched stems

Fruit: lopsided green berry, 1½-4" (4-10 cm) long, turning brown when ripe

Bloom: winter, spring

Cycle/Origin: perennial; native

Habitat: pinelands, open woods, fields, pastures

Range: northern and central Florida

Notes: Before the leaves appear on this handsome deciduous shrub, the showy flowers explode into bloom from the last year's buds. Up close, one can detect the subtle lemon scent from the blossoms. The leaves (especially the new growth) have an extremely hairy, almost velvety feeling to the touch, thus "Woolly" in the common name. The conspicuous flowers of this species (and those of all other pawpaws) are pollinated by beetles, and the resulting odd-shaped fruits are eaten by small mammals and wild turkeys.

FLOWER TYPE	LEAF TYPE	LEAF ATTACHMENT	FRUIT
Irregular	Simple	Alternate	Berry

ATAMASCO LILY
Zephyranthes atamasca

Family: Lily (Liliaceae)

Height: 5-12" (13-30 cm)

Flower: large funnel-shaped flower, 3-4" (7.5-10 cm) long, with 6 similar-looking, lance-shaped, pointed, white petals and sepals that are fused at their bases and broadly flaring at the mouth, and 6 flower parts (stamens) tipped with bright yellowish orange

Leaf: shiny basal leaves, 6-18" (15-45 cm) long, are smooth-edged, uniformly thin, and taper to a point at the tips

Bloom: winter, spring

Cycle/Origin: perennial; native

Habitat: moist soils, rich woodlands, wet meadows, moist roadside ditches

Range: northern and central Florida

Notes: Listed by the state of Florida as threatened, the showy white flowers of this delicate wildflower arise from an underground bulb. Blooming very early in the season, Atamasco Lily is a true harbinger of spring. Fond of wet rich soils, it often occurs in extensive colonies in bottomland forests and in moist areas along roads. Species name *atamasca* is derived from an American Indian word meaning "stained in blood" and refers to the white blossoms that are frequently tinged with pink. All parts of the plant are poisonous, one reason why it shouldn't be transplanted from the wild.

FLOWER TYPE **LEAF TYPE** **LEAF ATTACHMENT**

Tube **Simple** **Basal**

fruit

BLUESTEM PRICKLY POPPY
Argemone albiflora

Family: Poppy (Papaveraceae)

Height: 1-4' (30-122 cm)

Flower: showy cup-shaped flower, 3-4½" (7.5-11 cm) wide, composed of 6 large but thin, wrinkled, pure white petals surrounding a round, yellowish orange center

Leaf: lance-shaped, bluish green leaves, 3-8" (7.5-20 cm) long, are lobed with wavy spiny margins; leaves alternately clasp a thorny, thick, upright, branched stem

Fruit: upright spiny green pod, 1-1½" (2.5-4 cm) long, turning brown at maturity

Bloom: spring, summer, fall

Cycle/Origin: annual, biennial; native

Habitat: dry disturbed sites, roadsides, pastures, old fields

Range: northern and central Florida

Notes: A distinctive and formidable-looking wildflower, its bluish green leaves are well armored with sharp spines and its stems are thorny, thus the suitable common name of Bluestem Prickly Poppy. Providing an ample source of pollen, the showy blooms attract foraging bees. The plant contains yellow sap. All parts of the plant are toxic and may even be fatal if ingested.

FLOWER TYPE	LEAF TYPE	LEAF ATTACHMENT	LEAF ATTACHMENT	FRUIT
Regular	Simple Lobed	Alternate	Clasping	Pod

PERFUMED SPIDER LILY
Hymenocallis latifolia

Family: Lily (Liliaceae)

Height: 3-4' (.9-1.2 m)

Flower: large tubular white flower, 3½-8" (9-20 cm) long, with 6 petals, 3-5" (7.5-13 cm) long, that are narrow and abruptly bend downward, below a funnel-shaped membrane that connects the bases of 6 long arching flower parts (stamens); flowers in groups on long fleshy stalks

Leaf: thick narrow evergreen basal leaves, 18-36" (45-91 cm) long, are shiny, smooth, upright and arch from the base

Fruit: oval, pale green-to-tan capsule, 1-2" (2.5-5 cm) wide; chambered, it houses large flat black seeds

Bloom: spring, summer, fall

Cycle/Origin: perennial; native

Habitat: coastal sites, mangrove swamps, dune margins

Range: central and southern Florida

Notes: Distinctive ribbon-like petals of the fragrant showy flowers dangle like the legs of a spider, giving the plant part of its common name. The long and fleshy, arching leaves that grow from an underground bulb resemble those of an amaryllis on steroids. Perfumed Spider Lily is a fast-growing, clump-forming, easy-to-grow plant that is also salt and drought tolerant, making it a popular choice for any coastal garden. Native to southern Florida and West Indies.

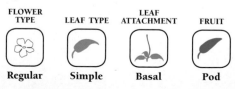

FLOWER TYPE	LEAF TYPE	LEAF ATTACHMENT	FRUIT
Regular	Simple	Basal	Pod

STARRUSH WHITETOP
Rhynchospora colorata

Family: Sedge (Cyperaceae)

Height: 12-24" (30-61 cm)

Flower: round cluster, ¼-⅓" (.6-.8 cm) wide, of many small, cone-shaped structures (called spikelets); 3-6 narrow long bracts (often mistaken for petals) are just below the spikelets; each bract, 1-3" (2.5-7.5 cm) long, is white with a green tip and abruptly bends downward; cluster and bracts atop a triangular stem

Leaf: uniformly thin and grass-like green leaves, 4-6" (10-15 cm) long, are smooth; leaves mostly basal; stem leaves are smaller and alternate up the stem

Bloom: spring, summer, fall

Cycle/Origin: perennial; native

Habitat: moist pinelands, wet prairies or ditches

Range: throughout

Notes: A conspicuous component of various open wet habitats throughout Florida, Starrush Whitetop is actually a flowering, grass-like sedge. What at first glance appear to be petals are actually long, white, petal-like bracts with green tips. The bracts radiate outward from just below the round cluster of spikelets like a star, providing this graceful plant with parts of its common name. Spreads by underground stems (rhizomes) and often forms extensive colonies with flowers that dot the landscape with white.

CLUSTER TYPE	FLOWER TYPE	LEAF TYPE	LEAF ATTACHMENT	LEAF ATTACHMENT
Round	**Irregular**	**Simple**	**Alternate**	**Basal**

ARRASA CON TODO
Gomphrena serrata

Family: Amaranth (Amaranthaceae)

Height: 2-6" (5-15 cm)

Flower: round to short elongated cluster, ¼-⅓" (.6-.8 cm) wide, of small tubular cottony white flowers; each flower is surrounded by 2 papery white bracts

Leaf: hairy lance-shaped leaves, ½-2½" (1-6 cm) long, are oppositely attached to a sprawling or ascending stem

Bloom: year-round

Cycle/Origin: annual, perennial; non-native

Habitat: dry disturbed sites, roadsides, lawns, fields, open woods

Range: throughout

Notes: Native to the American tropics, this low-growing annual has naturalized along the Gulf and Atlantic coasts in the United States. An inhabitant of open sandy sites and often encountered along roads and sidewalks. The plant is considered a nuisance weed of lawns, fields and other landscaped areas. In fact, the common name is Spanish and roughly translated means "destroys everything." Also called Prostrate Globe Amaranth, it is a close relative of the familiar and more ornamental container or window box annual commonly sold in garden centers.

CLUSTER TYPE	FLOWER TYPE	LEAF TYPE	LEAF ATTACHMENT
Round	Tube	Simple	Opposite

fruit

BUTTON-SAGE
Lantana involucrata

Family: Verbena (Verbenaceae)

Height: 3-6' (.9-1.8 m); shrub

Flower: flat cluster, ½-¾" (1-2 cm) wide, of several small tubular white flowers with a yellow center; each flower has 5 lobes widely flaring at the mouth

Leaf: pale green-to-green oval leaves, ¾-1" (2-2.5 cm) long, have slightly scalloped margins, are rough to the touch and have a sage-like smell; oppositely attached to a multi-branched woody stem

Fruit: small berry-like green fruit, ¼" (.6 cm) wide, turns purple when ripe

Bloom: year-round

Cycle/Origin: perennial; native

Habitat: pinelands, forest edges, coastal areas, disturbed sites

Range: central and southern Florida

Notes: A common woody shrub of the American tropics. Like its more colorful and easily recognized relative Lantana (pg. 97), Button-sage is a sun-loving, densely branched plant with rough, aromatic leaves. Although small and not overly showy, the white flower heads are quite popular with butterflies. A tough plant that can tolerate salt spray and very dry conditions. Tea brewed from the leaves has been used to treat high blood pressure or colic, and has even been used topically to relieve itchy skin or sores resulting from measles or chicken pox.

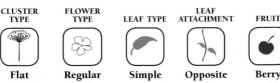

CLUSTER TYPE	FLOWER TYPE	LEAF TYPE	LEAF ATTACHMENT	FRUIT
Flat	Regular	Simple	Opposite	Berry

SPOTTED BEE BALM
Monarda punctata

Family: Mint (Lamiaceae)

Height: 12-36" (30-91 cm)

Flower: spike cluster of ragged whorls, ½-¾" (1-2 cm) wide, of lance-shaped, downward-curving, greenish white-to-purple bracts and purple-dotted, cream-colored flowers; each flower, ¾-1" (2-2.5 cm) long, has 5 petals (2 in upper lip and 3 in larger lower lip); bracts and flowers alternate along upper part of stem

Leaf: lance-shaped green leaves, 1-3" (2.5-7.5 cm) long, finely toothed edges; oppositely attached to branched hairy square stem

Bloom: summer, fall

Cycle/Origin: perennial; native

Habitat: sandy disturbed sites, dry open woodlands, forest margins, old fields, along roads

Range: throughout Florida, except in the extreme southern portion of the state

Notes: This clump-forming wildflower provides abundant, late season color. The conspicuous, leaf-like bracts vary from greenish white to white to purple and overshadow the actual small flowers with arching, cream-colored petals. Species name *punctata* refers to the noticeably dotted petals, thus another common name, Dotted Horsemint. Its distinctive appearance and its ability to attract various pollinators make it a great addition to any native or wildlife garden.

CLUSTER TYPE	FLOWER TYPE	LEAF TYPE	LEAF ATTACHMENT
Spike	**Irregular**	**Simple**	**Opposite**

HAIRY-FRUITED CHERVIL
Chaerophyllum tainturieri

Family: Carrot (Apiaceae)

Height: 10-28" (25-71 cm)

Flower: small branched flat cluster, ½-1" (1-2.5 cm) wide, composed of 3-10 tiny white flowers, each with 5 oval petals surrounding a greenish yellow center

Leaf: hairy compound leaves, 1-5" (2.5-13 cm) long, are finely divided, giving an overall fern-like appearance; alternately attached to an upright hairy stem

Bloom: spring

Cycle/Origin: annual; native

Habitat: dry to moist soils, disturbed sites, roadsides, fields, forest margins

Range: northern and central Florida

Notes: After just a quick look at the fern-like leaves, it is clear that Hairy-fruited Chervil belongs to the Carrot family, as they resemble the greens of common garden carrots. Even the crushed stems and leaves emit a delightful carrot-like aroma, a characteristic of several members of the genus *Chaerophyllum*, a name blended from two Greek words that translate to mean "pleasant leaf." This plant has relatively flat-topped clusters (umbels) of white flowers, also typical of most Carrot family members. A widespread weedy annual, it spreads rapidly by seed and quickly colonizes a variety of open disturbed areas.

CLUSTER TYPE	FLOWER TYPE	LEAF TYPE	LEAF ATTACHMENT
Flat	Regular	Compound	Alternate

CLUSTERED BUSHMINT
Hyptis alata

Family: Mint (Lamiaceae)

Height: 2-8' (.6-2.4 m)

Flower: large round cluster, ½-1" (1-2.5 cm) wide, of many small, 2-lipped white flowers, subtly dotted with purple; flower heads have leafy green bracts below and grow from upper leaf attachments

Leaf: lance-shaped, dark green leaves, 1½-3½" (4-9 cm) long, with blunt-toothed edges and often a slightly wavy appearance; lower leaves have longer stalks than upper leaves; oppositely attached to a stout, upright, branched, purplish green stem

Bloom: summer, fall

Cycle/Origin: perennial; native

Habitat: moist soils, wet roadside ditches, moist pinelands, wetland margins

Range: throughout

Notes: The large round flower heads of this tall and conspicuous wildflower are numerous and take on a slightly ragged appearance, especially as they age. Its foliage emits a distinct musky odor when crushed, thus another common name, Muskymint. Like others in the Mint family, the stout stems are square. In addition, Clustered Bushmint stems take on an almost winged appearance. In fact, the species name *alata* is derived from a Latin word meaning "winged." When in bloom, its flowers are a favorite of small butterflies and bees.

CLUSTER TYPE	FLOWER TYPE	LEAF TYPE	LEAF ATTACHMENT
Round	Irregular	Simple	Opposite

bristles

EASTERN BACCHARIS
Baccharis halimifolia

Family: Aster (Asteraceae)

Height: 3-12' (.9-3.7 m)

Flower: tight round cluster, ¾-2" (2-5 cm) wide, of white flower heads, each ¼-½" (.6-1 cm) long, that are of disk flowers only and enclosed in overlapping bracts

Leaf: grayish green leaves, ¾-3" (2-7.5 cm) long, are oval to elliptical, evergreen and with coarsely toothed edges above the midpoints; largest near the plant base, becoming smaller and narrower upward; alternate on an upright, densely branched stem

Bloom: fall

Cycle/Origin: perennial; native

Habitat: open woodlands, forest edges, roadsides, old fields, coastal areas, salt marsh margins, easements

Range: throughout

Notes: Also known as Groundselbush, this abundant and late-flowering evergreen shrub has a rounded crown and a densely branched form. Highly salt tolerant and common in coastal habitats. Its small flowers are female or male and are produced on separate plants. Seeds of female flowers are topped with long and silky, dandelion-like white bristles (see inset), giving the female plants an overall fuzzy, cottony look. Male plants are slightly smaller and much less noticeable. The genus name *Baccharis* is for Bacchus, the Roman god of wine.

CLUSTER TYPE	FLOWER TYPE	LEAF TYPE	LEAF ATTACHMENT
Round	**Composite**	**Simple**	**Alternate**

SILVER CROTON
Croton argyranthemus

Family: Spurge (Euphorbiaceae)

Height: 10-24" (25-61 cm)

Flower: short spike cluster, ¾-2" (2-5 cm) long, composed of several small hairy white flowers; cluster is at the end of stem (terminal)

Leaf: elliptical leaves, ¾-1½" (2-4 cm) long, are green above and silvery or brownish green below, and have smooth margins; alternately attached to an upright brown stem

Bloom: spring, summer

Cycle/Origin: perennial; native

Habitat: pinelands, open woods, forest margins

Range: northern and central Florida

Notes: A small wildflower of dry forest habitats, Silver Croton is named for the dense hairs covering the lower surfaces of its leaves that give the plant an overall silvery appearance. Although not showy, it serves as host for the caterpillars of Goatweed Butterfly, a distinctive and reclusive Florida butterfly that has a cryptic, leaf-like brown pattern on the undersides of its wings. Historically, Silver Croton's clear sap was used to help treat cuts, scrapes and even skin cancer lesions, giving it another common name, Healing Croton.

CLUSTER TYPE	FLOWER TYPE	LEAF TYPE	LEAF ATTACHMENT
Spike	**Irregular**	**Simple**	**Alternate**

AQUATIC MILKWEED
Asclepias perennis

Family: Milkweed (Asclepiadaceae)

Height: 12-32" (30-80 cm)

Flower: domed flat cluster, 1-2" (2.5-5 cm) wide, of many white-to-pale pinkish white flowers; each flower, ¼" (.6 cm) wide, with 5 downward-curving petals and a deeply divided crown, made up of 5 scoop-shaped "hoods" and 5 inward-curving, beak-like "horns"

Leaf: narrow lance-shaped leaves, 2-6" (5-15 cm) long, dark green, short-stalked; thin, often branched stems

Fruit: elongated curved green pod, 1½-2½" (4-6 cm) long, narrow, tapering toward the tip; turns brown; splits open to release many dark brown seeds, each with cottony plumed tufts that carry it away on the wind

Bloom: spring, summer, fall

Cycle/Origin: perennial; native

Habitat: marshes, swamps, wet areas, ditches, river edges

Range: northern two-thirds of Florida

Notes: Aptly named, this compact, white-flowered milkweed is almost exclusively seen in or near wetlands. Despite its preference for moist conditions, it adapts well to most garden settings as long as it is watered regularly. It provides nectar for many pollinating insects and is a host for caterpillars of Monarch and Queen butterflies. The species name *perennis* means "through the year," referring to its long blooming period as compared to many other milkweeds.

CLUSTER TYPE	FLOWER TYPE	LEAF TYPE	LEAF ATTACHMENT	LEAF ATTACHMENT	FRUIT
Flat	Irregular	Simple	Opposite	Clasping	Pod

SEA LAVENDER
Argusia gnaphalodes

Family: Forget-me-not (Boraginaceae)

Height: 2-6' (.6-1.8 m)

Flower: small spike cluster, ½-3" (1-7.5 cm) long, curled under at the tip and packed with many 5-petaled white flowers with pale green centers; flowers in pairs along 1 side of spike, open from the base of the spike upward and turn pink to lavender with age

Leaf: slender, hairy, silvery-to-grayish green leaves, 1-4" (2.5-10 cm) long; alternate lower on stem, whorled at stem tip; dead gray leaves hang from fleshy branches that are low and spreading to upright

Bloom: year-round

Cycle/Origin: perennial; native

Habitat: sandy or rocky ocean shorelines and beaches

Range: southern Florida

Notes: Also called Sea Rosemary, this distinctive mounding shrub closely resembles a succulent at first glance. Specialized for life just above the wave zone of ocean shorelines, it is extremely drought and salt tolerant. Once common, it has lost much of its available habitat to coastal development and is now mostly limited to the southeastern Florida coast and the islands of the Florida Keys. Listed by the state as an endangered species. The small, single-seeded fruit has a corky outer layer that helps it to float and disperse widely.

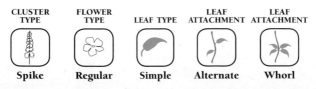

CLUSTER TYPE	FLOWER TYPE	LEAF TYPE	LEAF ATTACHMENT	LEAF ATTACHMENT
Spike	Regular	Simple	Alternate	Whorl

SCORPION'S TAIL
Heliotropium angiospermum

Family: Forget-me-not (Boraginaceae)

Height: 12-36" (30-91 cm); shrub

Flower: small spike cluster, ½-3" (1-7.5 cm) long, curling under at the tip and composed of many paired, 5-petaled, white flowers with pale yellow centers; flowers are along 1 side of spike and open from the base of spike upward

Leaf: hairy, lance-shaped, dark green leaves, 1-5½" (2.5-14 cm) long, are strongly veined, wrinkled and have smooth margins; alternately attached to an upright branched stem

Bloom: year-round

Cycle/Origin: perennial; native

Habitat: coastal sites, dry disturbed areas, shell mounds, roadsides

Range: central and southern Florida

Notes: Common mainly in southern Florida coastal counties, this compact woody shrub tolerates harsh conditions and dry rocky or sandy soils. The slender flower spike is coiled at the tip, resembling the menacing tail of a scorpion and providing the plant with its common name. Relatively short-lived, it produces an ample supply of seeds that quickly germinate in the surrounding landscape. Despite its inconspicuous flower spike, Scorpion's Tail is gaining popularity among native plant enthusiasts for use in butterfly gardens.

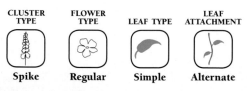

CLUSTER TYPE	FLOWER TYPE	LEAF TYPE	LEAF ATTACHMENT
Spike	Regular	Simple	Alternate

bulblets

MEADOW GARLIC
Allium canadense

Family: Lily (Liliaceae)

Height: 8-24" (20-61 cm)

Flower: flat cluster, 1-2½" (2.5-6 cm) wide, of few white-to-pinkish white flowers; each flower, ⅓-½" (.8-1 cm) wide, has 6 elliptical petals; flower cluster sits above the leaves atop a long upright smooth stalk

Leaf: uniformly narrow, grass-like basal leaves, 6-12" (15-30 cm) long

Bloom: spring

Cycle/Origin: perennial; native

Habitat: roadsides, old fields, disturbed sites

Range: northern and central Florida

Notes: The long, grass-like leaves of Meadow Garlic arise from a small underground bulb. The flower cluster at the end of the stalk produces several individual blooms as well as clusters of small aboveground bulbs, called bulblets. In fact, Meadow Garlic reproduces mostly by these bulbs and bulblets (few seeds are produced), and forms extensive colonies. Although "Garlic" is in the common name, the plant gives off a strong onion-like odor. The leaves, bulbs and bulblets are edible, but should be used in moderation as they have a much stronger flavor than traditional onions purchased in stores.

CLUSTER TYPE	FLOWER TYPE	LEAF TYPE	LEAF ATTACHMENT
Flat	**Regular**	**Simple**	**Basal**

CLIMBING HEMPVINE
Mikania scandens

Family: Aster (Asteraceae)

Height: 3-15' (.9-4.6 m); vine

Flower: dense flat-topped clusters, 1-3" (2.5-7.5 cm) wide, of many small, fuzzy, white-to-pale pink flower heads; each elongated flower head (umbel) is composed of 4 disk flowers only, lacking ray flowers; each cluster is borne on a long flower stalk

Leaf: heart-shaped leaves, 1-5" (2.5-13 cm) long, tapering sharply at the tips and with wavy or widely toothed margins, are on long leafstalks oppositely attached to a twining or sprawling stem

Bloom: summer, fall

Cycle/Origin: perennial; native

Habitat: roadsides, moist open woodlands, forest edges, wetland margins

Range: throughout

Notes: This is a common and somewhat weedy, aggressive twining vine of moist habitats. Displaying a rather sprawling nature, it rambles up and over the top of surrounding low vegetation. In late summer and autumn, Climbing Hempvine explodes with a showy display of fuzzy flower clusters that are usually teeming with a wide variety of insects such as bees, flies and butterflies. From a distance, the clusters appear white, but upon closer inspection, the open flowers look pale pink.

CLUSTER TYPE	FLOWER TYPE	LEAF TYPE	LEAF ATTACHMENT	LEAF ATTACHMENT
Flat	Composite	Simple	Alternate	Opposite

CAROLINA REDROOT
Lachnanthes caroliana

Family: Bloodwort (Haemodoraceae)

Height: 12-32" (30-80 cm)

Flower: large rounded flat cluster, 1½-3" (4-7.5 cm) wide, of small, woolly, dull white flowers, each ½" (1 cm) long, with protruding yellow flower parts (stamens)

Leaf: long and uniformly narrow, grayish green leaves tapering to points; basal leaves, 6-18" (15-45 cm) long, overlap at the base of stem; stem leaves are much shorter and clasping

Bloom: spring, summer, fall

Cycle/Origin: perennial; native

Habitat: wet sites, roadside ditches, marshes, bogs, moist pinelands, wet prairies, swamp margins

Range: throughout

Notes: The common name in part is for the bright red roots and horizontal underground stems (rhizomes), said to be food for Sandhill Cranes. The long sword-like leaves overlap at the base of the stem, much like the foliage of irises. When in bloom, however, Carolina Redroot is easy to differentiate from iris blossoms. The genus name *Lachnanthes*, derived from two Greek words combined and meaning "woolly flowers," refers to the unusual white blooms that attract many types of butterflies. Common in a wide variety of moist habitats, it is a wetland indicator species that spreads rapidly and is capable of forming dense and expansive colonies.

CLUSTER TYPE	FLOWER TYPE	LEAF TYPE	LEAF ATTACHMENT	LEAF ATTACHMENT
Flat	Irregular	Simple	Clasping	Basal

SWEET EVERLASTING
Pseudognaphalium obtusifolium

Family: Aster (Asteraceae)

Height: 8-36" (20-91 cm)

Flower: ragged flat cluster, 1-4" (2.5-10 cm) wide, of several barrel-shaped flower heads, each ¼" (.6 cm) long; flower heads made up of yellow or orange disk flowers surrounded by rough woolly white bracts

Leaf: narrow lance-shaped leaves, 1-3" (2.5-7.5 cm) long, are stalkless, with few hairs above and dense white hairs below that give the leaves an overall silvery appearance; leaves are numerous and alternately attached to a slender, greenish white stem

Bloom: fall

Cycle/Origin: annual, biennial; native

Habitat: disturbed sites, roadsides, old fields, pastures, open woods, dry areas

Range: throughout

Notes: A distinctive, late-season wildflower readily identified by its silvery foliage and densely woolly, fragrant flower heads. If cut early, the blooms can be dried and used in floral arrangements. Also called Rabbit-tobacco, this plant was used widely by American Indians. The smoke from the dried leaves was thought to hold many spiritual and restorative powers, and it helped cure a variety of respiratory ailments. It was also used topically to help treat bruises, cuts and wounds.

CLUSTER TYPE

Flat

FLOWER TYPE

Composite

LEAF TYPE

Simple

LEAF ATTACHMENT

Alternate

SUMMER FAREWELL
Dalea pinnata

Family: Pea or Bean (Fabaceae)

Height: 18-36" (45-91 cm)

Flower: showy flat cluster, 1½-3½" (4-9 cm) wide, composed of small, rounded, dense, fuzzy white flower heads, ½" (1 cm) wide; flower heads have prominent reddish brown bracts below; cluster at the ends of stem

Leaf: compound leaves, finely divided into numerous (can be 3 to many) small, needle-like leaflets; each leaflet, ¼-⅓" (.6-.8 cm) long; leaves are alternately attached to slender arching stems

Bloom: summer, fall

Cycle/Origin: perennial; native

Habitat: dry sandy sites, pinelands, along roads

Range: northern and central Florida

Notes: Well adapted to sandy dry habitats, this delicate wildflower of the Southeast produces large, multi-stemmed clumps of slender arching stems. Aptly named, Summer Farewell explodes into bloom with showy, pure white flower heads, as if affording the summer season with one last hurrah before the onset of autumn. The species name *pinnata* refers to the finely cut, slender leaflets that give the plant an overall lacy appearance. A frequent host for the hungry caterpillars of Southern Dogface, Florida's only sulphur butterfly with pointed forewings.

CLUSTER TYPE	FLOWER TYPE	LEAF TYPE	LEAF ATTACHMENT
Flat	Irregular	Compound	Alternate

DIXIE WHITETOP ASTER
Sericocarpus tortifolius

Family: Aster (Asteraceae)

Height: 12-36" (30-91 cm)

Flower: small flat cluster, 1½-4" (4-10 cm) wide, composed of several shaggy, daisy-like flower heads, each ⅜-⅔" (.9-1.6 cm) wide, with only 2-5 pure white petals (ray flowers) surrounding a white center (disk flowers); flower heads on short flower stalks

Leaf: hairy oval leaves, ½-1½" (1-4 cm) long, with smooth edges and slightly pointed tips; stalkless and alternately attached to a slender upright stem

Bloom: summer, fall

Cycle/Origin: perennial; native

Habitat: sandy sites, pinelands, dry woodlands, old fields

Range: throughout

Notes: A common wildflower of sandy pinelands and scrublands, this late-season perennial is one of only two members of the *Sericocarpus* genus in Florida. The slightly ragged flower heads give rise to seeds with very prominent, silky white hairs that give the flower cluster an overall fuzzy appearance. The hairs help the seeds disperse in the wind. Species name *tortifolius* is derived from two Latin words combined to mean "twisted leaves," referring to the subtle, but distinctive growth of the foliage.

CLUSTER TYPE
Flat

FLOWER TYPE
Composite

LEAF TYPE
Simple

LEAF ATTACHMENT
Alternate

VIRGIN'S BOWER
Clematis virginiana

Family: Buttercup (Ranunculaceae)

Height: 6-10' (1.8-3 m); vine

Flower: delicate round cluster, 2-4" (5-10 cm) wide, of white flowers; each flower, 1" (2.5 cm) wide, with 4-5 petal-like sepals and a center of many thin, hair-like, greenish yellow flower parts (stamens)

Leaf: 3-parted compound leaves; each leaflet, 2" (5 cm) long, is sharply toothed or lobed

Bloom: summer, fall

Cycle/Origin: perennial; native

Habitat: woodland margins, fence rolls, moist woods

Range: northern and central Florida

Notes: Virgin's Bower is one of nearly 20 species of *Clematis* found growing in eastern North America. A close relative of the garden clematis, this square-stemmed perennial vine usually is seen growing over fences or shrubs or along riverbanks. Late in summer and fall, the hairy plumes of its pollinated female flowers look like a frosted vine. The seed heads have curvy, hair-like white projections, giving the plant the appearance of the beard of an elderly man and giving rise to another common name, Old Man's Beard. Can be grown from seed.

CLUSTER TYPE	FLOWER TYPE	LEAF TYPE	LEAF ATTACHMENT
Round	Regular	Compound	Opposite

VIRGINIA PEPPERWEED
Lepidium virginicum

Family: Mustard (Brassicaceae)

Height: 12-24" (30-61 cm)

Flower: dense spike cluster, 1-6" (2.5-15 cm) long, of numerous tiny, 4-petaled, white flowers with yellow flower parts (anthers); many spikes per plant

Leaf: lance-shaped leaves, 1-2½"(2.5-6 cm) long, with smooth or toothed margins; stem leaves are many, alternate and clasping an upright, widely branched stem; basal leaves (usually absent at flowering time) are longer, deeply lobed and in a rosette

Bloom: year-round

Cycle/Origin: annual, biennial; native

Habitat: disturbed sites, along roads, croplands, fields

Range: throughout

Notes: Seemingly found at just about every roadside and other dry disturbed sites throughout much of the United States. The young leaves of Virginia Pepperweed are edible raw or cooked, highly nutritious and rich in vitamin C. Its small rounded fruits (called silicles) have a strong peppery taste and give rise to another common name, Poor Man's Pepper. The plant has a wide range of medicinal properties. It has been used as a diuretic and to help treat scurvy, coughs and asthma. A host plant for caterpillars of Checkered White and Great Southern White butterflies.

CLUSTER TYPE	FLOWER TYPE	LEAF TYPE	LEAF TYPE	LEAF ATTACHMENT	LEAF ATTACHMENT
Spike	**Regular**	**Simple**	**Simple Lobed**	**Alternate**	**Basal**

273

HAMMOCK SNAKEROOT
Ageratina jucunda

Family: Aster (Asteraceae)

Height: 12-36" (30-91 cm)

Flower: flat cluster, 2-6" (5-15 cm) wide, composed of numerous all-white flower heads, each with only disk flowers; petals (ray flowers) lacking; flower heads on short flower stalks from branched stems

Leaf: lance-shaped leaves, ¾-2½" (2-6 cm) long, are slightly triangular, have sharp-toothed edges and are on leafstalks that are oppositely attached to an upright (sometimes lax ascending) stem

Bloom: late summer, fall, winter

Cycle/Origin: perennial; native

Habitat: sandy soils, pinelands, dry woodlands, old fields, disturbed sites, dunes

Range: throughout Florida, except the western panhandle

Notes: Common and late-blooming with showy, slightly fragrant flower heads. The white heads shine brightly in dappled sunlight against the understory (the shaded foliage layer under a canopy of trees), as if illuminating the forest. In fact, "Hammock" in the common name refers to one of its habitats. Hammocks, which are found mainly in the southern United States, are forested small hills or knolls found next to marshy areas. *Jucunda* is from Latin and means "pleasing," a perfect species name for this lovely plant. Appears to respond well to disturbance and often forms extensive colonies.

CLUSTER TYPE

Flat

FLOWER TYPE

Composite

LEAF TYPE

Simple

LEAF ATTACHMENT

Opposite

leaves

BROADLEAF ARROWHEAD
Sagittaria latifolia

Family: Water-plantain (Alismataceae)

Height: aquatic

Flower: white spike cluster, 4-6" (10-15 cm) long, of whorls of 3 flowers; each flower, ½-1" (1-2.5 cm) wide, has 3 oval white-to-green petals around a center; cluster is on an upright stalk

Leaf: large toothless arrowhead-shaped leaves, 5-16" (13-40 cm) long, with strong veins; each leaf is held above the water on its own leafstalk; stems arise from the base of plant

Bloom: spring, summer, fall

Cycle/Origin: perennial; native

Habitat: wet areas, marshes, swamps, pond margins, wet ditches

Range: throughout

Notes: This distinctive wildflower is named for the arrowhead shape of its large expanded leaves. The leaves are held above the water surface, unlike the floating leaves of water lilies. It grows in the muddy bottoms of calm waters and produces edible tubers consumed by a variety of wildlife. A favorite food of large waterfowl such as geese, and of ducks—hence its other common name, Duck Potato. The tubers, also called *wapatoo*, have long been gathered by people for food.

CLUSTER TYPE
Spike

FLOWER TYPE
Regular

LEAF TYPE
Simple Lobed

LEAF ATTACHMENT
Basal

DOGTONGUE BUCKWHEAT
Eriogonum tomentosum

Family: Buckwheat (Polygonaceae)

Height: 12-36" (30-91 cm)

Flower: large showy flat cluster, 2-12" (5-30 cm) wide, composed of many white-to-pinkish white flowers; each flower lacks petals, but has 6 petal-like sepals

Leaf: glossy and dark green leaves; basal leaves, 4-6" (10-15 cm) long, are on short stalks; stalkless stem leaves, 1-2½" (2.5-6 cm) long, in whorls of 3-4 around hairy, upright and often branched stem; all leaves are densely hairy below, giving an overall white or tan appearance

Bloom: year-round

Cycle/Origin: perennial; native

Habitat: dry open woodlands, pinelands

Range: northern and central Florida

Notes: "Dogtongue" in the common name refers to the large and rounded basal leaves that resemble the shape of a canine's tongue. Also called Sandhill Wild Buckwheat, this showy wildflower occurs in dry pinelands and sandhills throughout the South Atlantic Coastal Plain from Florida to North Carolina. It thrives in open areas, benefiting from natural or prescribed fire, when there is limited competition from other herbaceous or woody plants. The large flower clusters attract a great variety of butterflies and other insects.

CLUSTER TYPE	FLOWER TYPE	LEAF TYPE	LEAF ATTACHMENT	LEAF ATTACHMENT
Flat	Regular	Simple	Whorl	Basal

FLYWEED
Bejaria racemosa

Family: Heath (Ericaceae)

Height: 2-8' (.6-2.4 m); shrub

Flower: large spike cluster, 6-9" (15-23 cm) long, of star-shaped white (often tinged with pink) flowers; each flower has sepals (calyx), 7 elliptical petals and numerous long flower parts (stamens)

Leaf: oval to elliptical leaves, ½-2" (1-5 cm) long, are thick and leathery with smooth edges; leaves (often pointing upward) are alternately attached to an upright, loosely branched, woody stem

Fruit: oval, 5-chambered, green capsule, ¼" (.6 cm) wide; turning brown with age and releasing many seeds

Bloom: summer, fall

Cycle/Origin: annual; native

Habitat: dry to moist soils, pinelands

Range: throughout Florida, except the western panhandle

Notes: When not in bloom, this common woody shrub is nondescript, but when flowering, the white spidery blossoms are eye-catching from afar and make the plant worthy of a closer look. Flower buds and sepals (calyx) exude a sticky liquid that flows down over the upper branches and traps insects, often in large numbers. The substance is as strong as the adhesives now used commercially for flypaper, resulting in plant's other common names, Flypaper or Tarflower. Historically, the plant was indeed used as a flypaper.

CLUSTER TYPE	FLOWER TYPE	LEAF TYPE	LEAF ATTACHMENT	FRUIT
Spike	Regular	Simple	Alternate	Pod

WHITE SWEET CLOVER
Melilotus alba

Family: Pea or Bean (Fabaceae)

Height: 3-6' (.9-1.8 m)

Flower: long spike cluster, 8" (20 cm) long, of pea-like white flowers, ¼" (.6 cm) long; each spike cluster grows on a short stalk

Leaf: compound leaves with 3 narrow, toothed, lance-shaped leaflets; each leaflet, ½-1" (1-2.5 cm) long

Fruit: egg-shaped pod

Bloom: year-round

Cycle/Origin: annual, biennial; non-native

Habitat: wet or dry soils, disturbed sites, roadsides, open fields, sun

Range: throughout

Notes: A non-native plant introduced from Europe via Eurasia, White Sweet Clover was once grown as a hay crop, but has escaped and now grows throughout the United States and Canada along roads and fields. This very fragrant plant smells like vanilla when its leaves or tiny flowers are crushed. The genus name *Melilotus* is Greek for "honey," referring to its use as a nectar source for bees. The bounty of white blossoms are also visited by a wide range of small butterflies, especially hairstreaks. Seeds can lie dormant in the soil for decades until the earth is disturbed and seeds come to within 7 inches (18 cm) of the surface. The amount of light in that depth of soil is enough to trigger germination.

CLUSTER TYPE	FLOWER TYPE	LEAF TYPE	LEAF ATTACHMENT	FRUIT
Spike	Irregular	Compound	Alternate	Pod

fruit

POKEWEED
Phytolacca americana

Family: Pokeweed (Phytolaccaceae)

Height: 4-10' (1.2-3 m)

Flower: distinctive long upright spike, 6-10" (15-25 cm) long, composed of many white flowers; each flower, ¼" (.6 cm) wide, has 5 petal-like sepals

Leaf: lance-shaped leaves, 5-10" (13-25 cm) long, that taper at both ends; alternately attached to a multi-branched, purplish red stem

Fruit: drooping clusters of dark purple-to-black berries on a distinctive red stem

Bloom: summer, fall

Cycle/Origin: perennial; native

Habitat: disturbed sites, forest margins, fields, clearings in woodlands

Range: throughout

Notes: A large and obvious plant with a history of many uses. Emerging shoots in spring were once gathered and cooked. In the nineteenth century, Pokeweed berry (known as pokeberry) juice was used as a dye and as ink. Many letters were written with "poke" juice during the Civil War. The berries are poisonous and should never be eaten by humans, but are readily consumed by numerous species of songbirds and several types of small mammals. As the plant matures, its leaves and shoots also become toxic and should not be eaten. The smooth green leaves turn a vibrant purplish red in autumn.

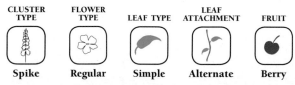

CLUSTER TYPE	FLOWER TYPE	LEAF TYPE	LEAF ATTACHMENT	FRUIT
Spike	Regular	Simple	Alternate	Berry

in seed

YANKEEWEED
Eupatorium compositifolium

Family: Aster (Asteraceae)

Height: 2-5' (61-152 cm)

Flower: elongated dense spike cluster, 5-18" (13-45 cm) long, of numerous tiny, greenish white flower heads made up entirely of disk flowers (lacking ray flowers); cluster is rarely drooping

Leaf: green leaves, deeply divided into numerous long and narrow segments, ½-3¼" (1-8 cm) long, are attached to an upright, freely branching stem; leaves are opposite at or near the stem base and alternate on the upper portion of stem

Bloom: summer, fall

Cycle/Origin: perennial; native

Habitat: disturbed sites, old fields, pastures, open woods

Range: throughout

Notes: The large, upright, white-flowering clumps of Yankeeweed are prominent features of the autumn landscape in Florida. It is similar-looking to Dog-fennel (pg. 299), but Yankeeweed is typically shorter in stature, has broader leaf segments and more compact, dense flower clusters. Both frequently occur together (often in large colonies) in open disturbed or recently burned sites. Unlike many other members of the genus that rely on insects for reproduction, both wispy flowering species are wind pollinated. Yankeeweed leaves are aromatic when crushed.

CLUSTER TYPE	FLOWER TYPE	LEAF TYPE	LEAF ATTACHMENT	LEAF ATTACHMENT
Spike	Composite	Simple Lobed	Alternate	Opposite

BULLTONGUE ARROWHEAD
Sagittaria lancifolia

Family: Water-plantain (Alismataceae)

Height: aquatic

Flower: large spike cluster, 6-24" (15-61 cm) long, of whorls of 3 flowers; each flower, 1-1½" (2.5-4 cm) wide, with 3 separated broad white petals and a yellow center; male flowers on upper part and female blooms on lower part of the same long upright stalk

Leaf: shiny, leathery, broad or narrow, lance-shaped leaves, 8-16" (20-40 cm) long, with smooth edges; leaves on long leafstalks from the base of the plant, which is usually below the surface of the water

Bloom: year-round

Cycle/Origin: perennial; native

Habitat: marshes, pond margins, swamps, wet ditches

Range: throughout

Notes: Perhaps the most commonly encountered of the ten arrowhead species found in Florida. Usually grows partially submerged in shallow waters along pond edges, canals or other freshwater wetlands. Can reach a height of 6 feet (1.8 m), with conspicuous flower spikes towering over large shiny leaves. Spreads by horizontal underground stems (rhizomes) and often forms dense stands. This plant and many members of *Sagittaria* share another common name, Duck Potato, which refers to the edible, potato-like, vertical underground stem (called a corm) in which a plant stores food.

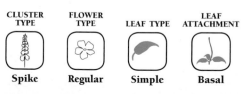

CLUSTER TYPE	FLOWER TYPE	LEAF TYPE	LEAF ATTACHMENT
Spike	Regular	Simple	Basal

fruit

WHITE WILD INDIGO
Baptisia alba

Family: Pea or Bean (Fabaceae)

Height: 2-5' (61-152 cm)

Flower: tall upright spike cluster, 12-18" (30-45 cm) long, of many large, pea-like, creamy white flowers, each ½-¾" (1-2 cm) long, opening from bottom of spike upward; spikes are above the foliage; few to many spikes per plant

Leaf: smooth, bluish green compound leaves, made up of 3 oval leaflets; each leaflet, 1-3" (2.5-7.5 cm) long; leaves attach to stout upright stems by short stalks

Fruit: hanging or drooping, oblong, beaked, inflated pod, ¾-1¾" (2-4.5 cm) long; green, turning black

Bloom: spring, summer

Cycle/Origin: perennial; native

Habitat: dry open woodlands, sandy disturbed sites

Range: northern and central Florida

Notes: This stately plant more closely resembles a shrub than a wildflower. The rounded, bushy and often multi-stemmed clumps give rise to long showy spikes of white flowers (favored by bumblebees) in spring. Although an extremely long-lived plant, it takes several years for it to become firmly established. Has a long taproot that helps it tolerate drought, fire and other disturbances. Readily available from specialty garden centers, it is a choice landscape perennial that provides an attractive floral and vegetative display.

CLUSTER TYPE	FLOWER TYPE	LEAF TYPE	LEAF ATTACHMENT	FRUIT
Spike	Irregular	Compound	Alternate	Pod

SAW PALMETTO
Serenoa repens

Family: Palm (Arecaceae)

Height: 4-7' (1.2-2.1 m); shrub

Flower: plume-like branched spike cluster, 12-24" (30-61 cm) long, composed of many small, 3-petaled, white-to-cream flowers

Leaf: fan-shaped, bluish green-to-green leaves, 24-36" (61-91 cm) long, with 20 uniformly narrow, pointed leaflets, each 16-30" (40-76 cm) long; leaves on long fine-toothed (saw-like) leafstalks

Fruit: large clusters of small oval green berries, each ½-¾" (1-2 cm) long; berries turn orange, then ripen to black or dark purple

Bloom: spring, summer

Cycle/Origin: perennial; native

Habitat: sandy soils, pinelands, dry woodlands

Range: throughout

Notes: A very common understory shrub with a sprawling trunk (sometimes more than one) and a rounded crown of large, fan-shaped leaves. Often forms large dense thickets that can be difficult to impossible to penetrate. The fragrant flowers attract insects and are source of nectar for high-grade honey. The berries are an important food for many bird and small mammal species. A berry extract is used to help treat prostate disorders, and urinary and bladder infections. Host to Palmetto Skipper butterflies and their caterpillars.

CLUSTER TYPE	FLOWER TYPE	LEAF TYPE	LEAF ATTACHMENT	FRUIT
Spike	Regular	Palmate	Alternate	Berry

fruit

SHYLEAF
Aeschynomene americana

Family: Pea or Bean (Fabaceae)

Height: 3-6' (.9-1.8 m)

Flower: small pea-like flower, ¼-⅓" (.6-.8 cm) wide, with petals varying in color from brownish yellow to pinkish orange and with a red and yellow throat: flowers in loose, often branched groups from the upper leaf attachments (axis)

Leaf: dark green compound leaves, 1-3" (2.5-7.5 cm) long, divided into numerous oblong paired leaflets; leaves alternately attached to a stout upright stem

Fruit: elongated flattened green pod, ¾-1½" (2-4 cm) long, turning brown, with scalloped segments; each segment contains 1 seed

Bloom: summer, fall

Cycle/Origin: annual; native

Habitat: moist open habitats, disturbed sites, forest margins, pond edges, wet ditches

Range: throughout

Notes: A tall plant of moist habitats that will even tolerate periodic flooding. Often forms dense stands and readily reseeds. The small feathery leaflets slowly fold up if disturbed, thus the common name. Widely grown as a warm-season forage for deer, wild turkeys and other game. Host for caterpillars of Barred Sulphur, a small yellow butterfly that looks distinctly different according to the season.

FLOWER TYPE	LEAF TYPE	LEAF ATTACHMENT	FRUIT
Irregular	Compound	Alternate	Pod

CREEPING WOOD SORREL
Oxalis corniculata

Family: Wood Sorrel (Oxalidaceae)

Height: 2-8" (5-20 cm)

Flower: small funnel-shaped yellow flower, ¼-½" (.6-1 cm) long, with 5 petals, is borne singly or in small clusters from upper leaf attachment (axis)

Leaf: clover-like compound leaves with 3 heart-shaped leaflets, ½-¾" (1-2 cm) wide; leaflets are attached at the tips; leaves are alternately attached by long leafstalks to slender, upright or reclining stems

Bloom: year-round

Cycle/Origin: perennial; native

Habitat: disturbed sites, lawns, roadsides, pastures, open woodlands, fields

Range: throughout

Notes: Creeping Wood Sorrel is a weedy, early invader of open disturbed areas. The heart-shaped leaves closely resemble those of clover and often fold up during the midday heat. The leaves have a sour taste due to the fact they contain high amounts of oxalic acid. This very small, low-growing, upright to trailing wildflower spreads by underground stems (rhizomes) and is capable of forming extensive dense mats. Colonizes new sites by seed, which are consumed and dispersed by a variety of songbirds.

FLOWER TYPE	LEAF TYPE	LEAF ATTACHMENT
Regular	**Compound**	**Alternate**

SIDEBEAK PENCILFLOWER
Stylosanthes biflora

Family: Pea or Bean (Fabaceae)

Height: 4-20" (10-50 cm)

Flower: pea-like, bright yellow flowers, ¼-½" (.6-1 cm) long, with 5 petals; solitary flower arises from leaf attachment (axis) at the end of stalk

Leaf: compound leaves, ⅝-1½" (1.5-4 cm) long, with 3 lance-shaped leaflets; each leaflet bears short bristles at the tip and along the margins; leaves alternately attached to rigid, often branched stem

Bloom: spring, summer, fall

Cycle/Origin: perennial; native

Habitat: sandy disturbed sites, dry open woodlands, pinelands, sandhills, forest margins

Range: northern two-thirds of Florida

Notes: An unassuming, sprawling or upright wildflower with stiff and wiry stems. Like other legumes, it is able to fix nitrogen from the air into the soil with the assistance of bacteria on the roots. Although common in dry open woodlands and other sandy sites, it may occasionally be found in moister habitats. Sidebeak Pencilflower is an important food source for native wildlife. Songbirds feed on the seeds, and deer and gopher tortoises forage on the leaves and other plant parts. A host plant for Barred Yellow butterfly caterpillars.

FLOWER TYPE	LEAF TYPE	LEAF ATTACHMENT
Irregular	**Compound**	**Alternate**

SENSITIVE PARTRIDGE PEA
Chamaecrista nictitans

Family: Pea or Bean (Fabaceae)

Height: 5-20" (13-50 cm)

Flower: bright yellow flower, ⅓-½" (.8-1 cm) wide, with 5 separate petals; lower petal is twice as long as upper petals; 1 or more flowers arise from each upper leaf attachment (axis)

Leaf: compound leaves, ¾-2" (2-5 cm) long, with 9-20 paired oblong leaflets and a distinct rounded nectar gland near the base; leaves alternately attached to an upright stem

Fruit: smooth flattened green pod, 1-2" (2.5-5 cm) long, turning brown at maturity; splits open to release small seeds

Bloom: spring, summer, fall

Cycle/Origin: annual; native

Habitat: disturbed areas, roadsides, old fields, hammock margins and openings

Range: throughout

Notes: Also called Wild Sensitive Plant, the small leaflets of this fern-like annual legume fold up when touched. A short shrubby plant that is common in dry woodlands and other open disturbed sandy sites. Spreads readily by seed. This wildflower and its showier relative, Partridge Pea (pg. 351), are important food sources for deer, various butterfly species and birds such as Northern Bobwhites.

FLOWER TYPE	LEAF TYPE	LEAF ATTACHMENT	FRUIT
Irregular	**Compound**	**Alternate**	**Pod**

fruit

RABBITBELLS
Crotalaria rotundifolia

Family: Pea or Bean (Fabaceae)

Height: 1-4" (2.5-10 cm)

Flower: pea-like, bright yellow flower, ⅓-½" (.8-1 cm) long, with 5 petals; 1 or a few flowers occur at the end of long upward-arching stalk

Leaf: compound leaves, with 3 rounded or elliptical leaflets, ½-1" (1-2.5 cm) long; leaves are hairy and alternately attached to a trailing stem

Fruit: smooth inflated cylindrical pod, ⅔-¾" (1.6-2 cm) long, with a thin pointed tip; green, turning brown at maturity; splits open to release bean-like seeds

Bloom: year-round

Cycle/Origin: perennial; native

Habitat: sandy roadsides, pinelands, sandhills

Range: throughout

Notes: Also called Prostrate Rattlebox for its creeping to almost mast-forming growth habit, this is a common perennial of dry sandy woodlands. Despite its widespread occurrence, the small pea-like flowers are easily overlooked. Nonetheless, it is a unique and under-used native perfect for a type of drought-tolerant landscaping known as xeriscaping. The dried, smooth, inflated pods have seeds inside and make a rattling noise when shaken, giving rise to the common name Rabbitbells. Like other *Crotalaria*, it contains pyrrolizidine alkaloids that render the entire plant (especially the seeds) poisonous.

FLOWER TYPE	LEAF TYPE	LEAF ATTACHMENT	FRUIT
Irregular	Compound	Alternate	Pod

COAT BUTTONS
Tridax procumbens

Family: Aster (Asteraceae)

Height: 6-8" (15-20 cm)

Flower: small solitary daisy-like flower, ½" (1 cm) wide, composed of a few 3-lobed, pale yellow-to-white petals (ray flowers) around a yellow center (disk flowers); flowers atop long upright flower stalks

Leaf: lance-shaped, dark green leaves, 1-6" (2.5-15 cm) long, are hairy and have toothed edges; oppositely attached to a hairy branched reclining stem

Bloom: year-round

Cycle/Origin: perennial; non-native

Habitat: disturbed sites, pastures, lawns, fields, roadsides, croplands

Range: central and southern Florida

Notes: Coat Buttons produces large quantities of wind-dispersed seeds that can travel far. Native to the American tropics, but has spread worldwide to become a noxious weed of countries with mild climates. The spreading branches arise from a main vertical root (taproot) and ramble low along the ground, often rooting at the leaf attachments (nodes) to form dense mats. Its small flowers shoot up from the plant on long stalks and are frequently visited by butterflies. The genus name *Tridax* means "three-toothed" and refers to the distinctive three-lobed flower petals. Considered a medicinal herb used to help treat cuts, wounds, pain, diarrhea and even asthma.

FLOWER TYPE	LEAF TYPE	LEAF ATTACHMENT
Composite	Simple	Opposite

fruit

BLADDER MALLOW
Herissantia crispa

Family: Mallow (Malvaceae)

Height: 12-36" (30-91 cm)

Flower: solitary, pale yellow-to-whitish yellow flower, ½-¾" (1-2 cm) wide, with 5 short broad petals around a yellow center; flower on long, angled stalk from the upper leaf attachment (axis)

Leaf: heart-shaped, grayish green-to-green leaves, ¾-2¾" (2-7 cm) long, are hairy with fine-toothed edges; alternately attached to a slender, somewhat sprawling stem

Fruit: inflated ribbed round capsule, ½-¾" (1-2 cm) wide, is green, turning papery brown at maturity; dangles from end of long "elbowed" stalk

Bloom: year-round

Cycle/Origin: annual, perennial; native

Habitat: coastal pinelands, hammocks, disturbed sites

Range: central and southern Florida

Notes: The small, less-than-showy flowers give rise to distinctive, bladder-like capsules that are reminiscent of Japanese lanterns. The capsules dangle from long, angled stalks and ornament the short plants. Also called Curly Abutilon, this is a common sprawling plant of mainly southern Florida coastal habitats. Host plant for caterpillars of Mallow Scrub-Hairstreak and Gray Hairstreak butterflies.

FLOWER TYPE	LEAF TYPE	LEAF ATTACHMENT	FRUIT
Regular	Simple	Alternate	Pod

fruit

CUBAN JUTE
Sida rhombifolia

Family: Mallow (Malvaceae)

Height: 2-5' (61-152 cm)

Flower: small flower, ½-¾" (1-2 cm) wide, with 5 whitish yellow-to-pale brownish yellow petals notched on 1 side of tips and fused at bases; single flowers on long "elbowed" flower stalks from upper leaf attachments

Leaf: lance-shaped to nearly diamond-shaped leaves, ¾-3" (2-7.5 cm) long, with toothed margins; undersides of leaves are hairy and grayish green; leaves alternate on slender upright multi-branched stem

Fruit: turban-shaped green pod, ¼" (.6 cm) wide, turns brown and splits at maturity to release many seeds

Bloom: year-round

Cycle/Origin: annual, perennial; native

Habitat: roadsides, old fields, disturbed sites, fields, open woodlands, forest margins

Range: throughout

Notes: Cuban Jute, with its long "elbowed" flower stalks, can be quickly distinguished from the similar-looking Common Wireweed (pg. 319), which has very short flower stalks. Widely used for its fibers and reputed to yield a natural product similar to true jute, thus "Jute" in its common name. However, not related to plants from which jute is produced. Historically, the leaves were smoked like tobacco or brewed as a tea for a stimulating, almost euphoric effect.

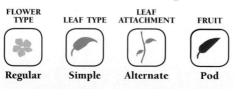

FLOWER TYPE · Regular   LEAF TYPE · Simple   LEAF ATTACHMENT · Alternate   FRUIT · Pod

WILD RADISH
Raphanus raphanistrum

Family: Mustard (Brassicaceae)

Height: 12-36" (30-91 cm)

Flower: small, pale yellow-to-white flower, ½-¾" (1-2 cm) wide, composed of 4 violet-veined broad petals around a yellow center; flowers occur in loose clusters at the end of stem

Leaf: dark green basal leaves, 6-8" (15-20 cm) long, are lyre-shaped with deep irregular lobes toward the base, toothed and hairy; stem leaves are smaller, slightly toothed or with smooth margins and alternately attached to a branched upright hairy stem

Fruit: long narrow green pod, 1-2½" (2.5-6 cm) long, points upward, has a pointed tip and is constricted between the seeds; pods turn brown at maturity

Bloom: spring

Cycle/Origin: annual; non-native

Habitat: roadsides, agricultural lands, waste areas

Range: throughout

Notes: Introduced from Europe and northern Asia, Wild Radish has naturalized throughout much of North America, where it has become an invasive, rapidly germinating, fast-growing weed of disturbed sites and croplands. Arising from an elongated taproot, it is a cool-season annual that usually dies back with the onset of warm Florida temperatures. The leaves and other plant parts are edible.

FLOWER TYPE	LEAF TYPE	LEAF TYPE	LEAF ATTACHMENT	LEAF ATTACHMENT	FRUIT
Regular	Simple	Simple Lobed	Alternate	Basal	Pod

NARROWLEAF SILKGRASS
Pityopsis graminifolia

Family: Aster (Asteraceae)

Height: 12-36" (30-91 cm)

Flower: few to many small, daisy-like, yellow flower heads, each ½-¾" (1-2 cm) wide, composed of several yellow petals (ray flowers) around a yellow center (disk flowers); groups of flowers are at the ends of multi-branched stems

Leaf: thin, pointed-tipped, grass-like leaves, 8-12" (20-30 cm) long; stem leaves smaller than basal leaves, and are alternately attached to the stiff upright stem; leaves and stem are covered with silky silvery hairs, giving an overall grayish green appearance

Bloom: summer, fall

Cycle/Origin: perennial; native

Habitat: dry sandy sites, pinelands, woodlands

Range: throughout

Notes: Easily identified by the silky hairs densely covering the leaves and stem, giving the plant an overall silvery or grayish green appearance. The species name *graminifolia* is derived from Latin and refers to the long, grass-like leaves. A distinctive wildflower, Narrowleaf Silkgrass has small, bright yellow flowers that provide a mass of late-season color. Often forms fairly dense and extensive colonies in the wild by underground stems (rhizomes) and by seed. The plant is a food resource for gopher tortoises.

FLOWER TYPE	LEAF TYPE	LEAF ATTACHMENT	LEAF ATTACHMENT
Composite	Simple	Alternate	Basal

SPINY SOW-THISTLE
Sonchus asper

Family: Aster (Asteraceae)

Height: 1-6' (.3-1.8 m)

Flower: dandelion-like, bright yellow flower head, ½-¾" (1-2 cm) wide; flower heads on flower stalks in loose groups atop long upright stems

Leaf: shiny, dark green leaves, 2½-12" (6-30 cm) long, with purple-to-creamy white midveins and wavy spiny margins; lower leaves deeply lobed, becoming less lobed and much smaller farther up the stem; leaves alternately attached and rounded bases clasp the stem

Bloom: spring, summer, fall

Cycle/Origin: annual; non-native

Habitat: disturbed sites, roadsides, agricultural lands

Range: throughout

Notes: Species name *asper* means "rough" and aptly describes this spiny, dangerous-looking plant. The thick leaves and stems exude a milky sap when broken. A native of Europe, this plant has naturalized throughout North America, where it is considered an undesirable weed of roadsides, pastures and other open disturbed landscapes. Common Sow-thistle (*S. oleraceus*) (not shown) is very similar, but has leaves that are noticeably less spiny. The mature seeds of Spiny Sow-thistle have silky, parachute-like white projections and are dispersed by the wind, thereby helping the spread of this invasive plant.

FLOWER TYPE

Composite

LEAF TYPE

Simple Lobed

LEAF ATTACHMENT

Alternate

LEAF ATTACHMENT

Clasping

fruit

SEPTICWEED
Senna occidentalis

Family: Pea or Bean (Fabaceae)

Height: 3-6' (.9-1.8 m)

Flower: 5-petaled, bright yellow flower, ½-1" (1.5-2.5 cm) wide; flowers occur in small groups from upper leaf attachment (axis)

Leaf: compound leaves, 8-12" (20-30 cm) long, are dark green, with 4-5 pairs of glossy pointed leaflets; each leaflet, 1¼-4" (3-10 cm) long; leaves are alternate on an upright, smooth, often branched stem

Fruit: flattened elongated curving pod, 4-8" (10-20 cm) long, is green and turns brown with age, splitting open to release many seeds

Bloom: summer, fall

Cycle/Origin: annual; non-native

Habitat: disturbed sites, old fields, agricultural lands

Range: throughout

Notes: This robust wildflower is a widespread tropical weed of disturbed sites and agricultural fields. Feed grain grown on land containing Septicweed can become contaminated, as parts of the plant are toxic to livestock and humans. It is superficially similar-looking to Coffeeweed (pg. 331), which has round-tipped leaflets, but Septicweed has glossy leaflets with pointed tips. The seeds of both species have been used as a coffee substitute after being roasted and ground, and are also reported to have a purgative effect.

FLOWER TYPE	LEAF TYPE	LEAF ATTACHMENT	FRUIT
Irregular	Compound	Alternate	Pod

COFFEEWEED
Senna obtusifolia

Family: Pea or Bean (Fabaceae)

Height: 6-36" (15-91 cm)

Flower: drooping, bright yellow flower, ½-1" (1-2.5 cm) wide, with 5 petals; small groups of flowers occur from the upper leaf attachment (axis)

Leaf: compound leaves made up of 2-3 pairs of leaflets; each paddle-shaped leaflet, ⅝-2" (1.5-5 cm) long, has a round tip; leaves are alternately attached to an upright, smooth, often branched stem

Fruit: elongated sickle-shaped pod, 4-8" (10-20 cm) long, is smooth and initially green, turning brown at maturity and splitting to release numerous seeds

Bloom: summer, fall

Cycle/Origin: annual; non-native

Habitat: disturbed areas, roadsides, old fields, fallow agricultural lands

Range: throughout

Notes: Native to tropical America, this is an exotic, bushy plant of open disturbed locations. The small seeds released from slender curving seedpods can persist in the soil for many years, waiting for the right conditions to germinate. The shape of the pods provide the basis for another common name, Sicklepod Senna. Despite their weedy natures, Coffeeweed and Septicweed (pg. 329) serve as host plants for Cloudless Sulphur and Sleepy Orange butterfly caterpillars.

FLOWER TYPE	LEAF TYPE	LEAF ATTACHMENT	FRUIT
Irregular	Compound	Alternate	Pod

BIGPOD SESBANIA
Sesbania herbacea

Family: Pea or Bean (Fabaceae)

Height: 3-10' (.9-3 m)

Flower: pea-like, bright yellow flower, ½-1" (1-2.5 cm) long, with upper petal (standard) mottled with red on the outside; flowers in few-flowered groups on long flower stalks from upper leaf attachments

Leaf: compound leaves, 6-12" (15-30 cm) long, with 24-70 oblong leaflets; each leaflet, ½-1" (1-2.5 cm) long; leaves alternate on a tall upright smooth stem

Fruit: long slender green pod, 6-10" (15-25 cm) long, turns brown and splits open to release many seeds

Bloom: summer, fall

Cycle/Origin: annual; native

Habitat: wetland edges, pond and canal margins, fields, disturbed sites

Range: throughout

Notes: A conspicuous weedy plant that can frequently reach a height of over 10 feet (3 m). Despite its often towering stature, the plant has an overall airy appearance due to the long, fern-like leaves that extend horizontally from the stem. The very long, slender pods (poisonous to humans) are many and persist on the plant after the leaves have dropped. Also known as Danglepod. Bigpod Sesbania was an important plant to American Indians, who obtained fibers from the stems for a variety of uses.

FLOWER TYPE	LEAF TYPE	LEAF ATTACHMENT	FRUIT
Irregular	**Compound**	**Alternate**	**Pod**

CAMPHORWEED
Heterotheca subaxillaris

Family: Aster (Asteraceae)

Height: 1-4' (30-122 cm)

Flower: small daisy-like flower head, ½-1" (1-2.5 cm) wide, made up of 20-45 golden yellow petals (ray flowers) surrounding a yellow center (disk flowers); flower heads in loose groups atop branches of stems; many flowers per plant

Leaf: hairy, oval to lance-shaped leaves, ¾-3½" (2-9 cm) long, with smooth or toothed edges; lower leaves are stalked and alternate, upper leaves are smaller and clasping; hairy, upright to ascending, multi-branched stem

Bloom: year-round

Cycle/Origin: annual, biennial; native

Habitat: dry sandy soils, pinelands, dry woods, pastures

Range: throughout

Notes: This rough-looking, weedy plant is a common sight along roads and other disturbed dry habitats throughout Florida. Although the golden flower heads are small, each plant produces many blossoms, resulting in an abundant display. The stems and leaves are sticky due to gland-tipped hairs. "Camphor" in the common name is for the camphor-like odor released from the foliage when crushed. The tiny seeds are consumed by a number of songbird species.

FLOWER TYPE

Composite

LEAF TYPE

Simple

LEAF ATTACHMENT

Alternate

LEAF ATTACHMENT

Clasping

fruit

HUSK-TOMATO
Physalis pubescens

Family: Nightshade (Solanaceae)

Height: 12-24" (30-61 cm)

Flower: solitary bell-shaped flower, ½-1" (1-2.5 cm) wide, with fused, pale yellow petals with dark purple at their bases; flowers on short leafstalks

Leaf: hairy leaves, 1¼-4" (3-10 cm) long, with coarse-toothed edges; alternately attached on stalks to a hairy upright stem

Fruit: small edible yellow berry, ½-⅔" (1-1.6 cm) wide, is inside an inedible papery inflated husk that looks like a lantern; the oval husk is green with prominent purple veins, then turns browns with age and often falls to the ground

Bloom: spring, summer

Cycle/Origin: annual; native

Habitat: pinelands, open woodlands, disturbed sites

Range: northern and central Florida

Notes: The small, pale yellow flowers give rise to berries enclosed in distinctive papery husks that resemble Japanese lanterns. The berries are sweet when ripe and make an excellent trailside snack or can be made into jam. Species name *pubescens* means "hairy," referring to the dense white hairs that cover the plant and give it an overall grayish green appearance.

FLOWER TYPE	LEAF TYPE	LEAF ATTACHMENT	FRUIT
Bell	Simple	Alternate	Berry

SLENDER SCRATCH DAISY
Croptilon divaricatum

Family: Aster (Asteraceae)

Height: 1-5' (30-152 cm)

Flower: small, all-yellow flower head, ¾-1" (2-2.5 cm) wide, composed of 7-11 elliptical petals (ray flowers) around a center of disk flowers; flower heads often on long flower stalks; many flower heads per plant

Leaf: uniformly thin leaves, 1-3" (2.5-7.5 cm) long, are smooth-edged or with a few sharp teeth; leaves become smaller upward on the plant; alternately attached to a slender upright and loosely branched, hairy stem

Bloom: summer, fall

Cycle/Origin: annual; native

Habitat: dry sandy soils, roadsides, disturbed sites, open dry woods, pinelands

Range: northern and central Florida

Notes: Also known as Goldenweed, this wispy wildflower is an aggressive, early invader of open sites with dry sandy soils. Spreads by wind-dispersed seed and can form dense colonies that provide electrically bright drifts of yellow in the landscape. Easily identified by its loosely branched form, slender hairy stem and the large number of small yellow flower heads. The species name *divaricatum* means "spreading apart," referring to the open, multi-branched structure of the plant. Previously in the genus *Haplopappus*.

FLOWER TYPE	LEAF TYPE	LEAF ATTACHMENT
Composite	Simple	Alternate

SMALL-FRUITED BEGGARTICKS
Bidens mitis

Family: Aster (Asteraceae)

Height: 1-5' (30-152 cm)

Flower: showy daisy-like flower head, ¾-1½" (2-4 cm) wide, of 8 or more elliptical, golden yellow petals (ray flowers) around a yellowish brown center (disk flowers); flowers are on long flower stalks

Leaf: long slender to lance-shaped, dark green leaves, 1½-4" (4-10 cm) long, are smooth-edged or deeply cut into several lobes and oppositely attached to a slender and smooth, upright, often branched stem

Bloom: late summer, fall

Cycle/Origin: annual; native

Habitat: wet soils, roadside ditches, disturbed sites, wetland margins

Range: throughout

Notes: Of the seven native *Bidens* species found in Florida, this plant and Romerillo (pg. 285) are the most commonly encountered. A lovely wildflower that adds waves of bright color late in the season to moist roadsides and wetlands throughout the state. Producing an abundance of barbed seeds that easily attach to clothing or animal fur, Small-fruited Beggarticks spreads rapidly and often occurs in expansive colonies. The showy golden flower heads attract bees and small butterflies. Seminole Indians used the plant to help treat a variety of ailments including diarrhea, headaches and fever.

FLOWER TYPE	LEAF TYPE	LEAF TYPE	LEAF ATTACHMENT
Composite	Simple	Simple Lobed	Opposite

JAMAICAN FEVERPLANT
Tribulus cistoides

Family: Caltrop (Zygophyllaceae)

Height: 3-8" (7.5-20 cm)

Flower: large solitary flower, 1-1½" (2.5-4 cm) wide, with 5 broad, bright yellow petals; flower on long flower stalk from the leaf attachment (axis)

Leaf: hairy compound leaves, 2-6" (5-15 cm) long, are dark green and divided into 6-10 pairs of elliptical leaflets; each leaflet, ½" (1 cm) long; leaves opposite on a hairy reclining stem

Fruit: spiny round green capsule, ½" (1 cm) wide, turns brown and splits with age; chambers within capsule

Bloom: year-round

Cycle/Origin: perennial; non-native

Habitat: coastal sites, beach dunes, disturbed areas

Range: central and southern Florida

Notes: A low-growing, extremely drought- and salt-tolerant weed often used as ground cover. The meanings of the genus name *Tribulus* and the family name Caltrop are synonymous. A caltrop is an ancient spiked weapon that was dropped on the ground to slow horses or enemy troops. Both names refer to the plant's spiny fruit capsules, which adhere to shoes, animal fur and even vehicle tires, thereby spreading its seeds. Also called Puncturevine. The spines can inflict a sharp pain to bare hands or feet. Ironically, the plant has been used medicinally as a pain reliever.

FLOWER TYPE	LEAF TYPE	LEAF ATTACHMENT	FRUIT
Regular	Compound	Opposite	Pod

347

MEXICAN PRIMROSE-WILLOW
Ludwigia octovalvis

Family: Evening-primrose (Onagraceae)

Height: 2-6' (.6-1.8 m)

Flower: large showy flower, 1-1½" (2.5-4 cm) wide, with 4 (rarely 5) broad, bright yellow petals that have slightly darker yellow spreading veins; petals are around a yellow center

Leaf: lance-shaped leaves, ¼-4" (2-10 cm) long, are green-to-greenish red with whitish red midveins and have smooth margins; multi-branched, green-to-reddish green stem; branches are hairy when young

Fruit: upright 4-angled capsule, ¼-2" (2-5 cm) long, tapering at the base, turning brown and splitting open at maturity to release numerous small seeds

Bloom: year-round

Cycle/Origin: perennial; native

Habitat: wet areas, pond and canal margins, swamp edges

Range: throughout

Notes: A common and shrubby native plant that is similar-looking to and often found growing alongside its more robust, non-native relative, Peruvian Primrose-willow (pg. 367). Mexican Primrose-willow is usually much shorter and has noticeably narrower leaves than Peruvian. Both species can dominate wetland areas by forming dense colonies. Species name *octovalvis* refers to the eight chambers or valves inside the cylindrical seed capsule.

FLOWER TYPE

Regular

LEAF TYPE

Simple

LEAF ATTACHMENT

Alternate

FRUIT

Pod

fruit

PARTRIDGE PEA
Chamaecrista fasciculata

Family: Pea or Bean (Fabaceae)

Height: 12-36" (30-91 cm)

Flower: bright yellow flower, 1-1½" (2.5-4 cm) wide, with 5 separate petals; 4 upper petals have a red base (one of the outer petals curves back to the center over the curving flower parts); 1 or more flowers arise from each upper leaf attachment (axis)

Leaf: compound leaves, 1¼-2½" (3-6 cm) long, with 6-18 paired oblong leaflets and a distinct rounded nectar gland near the base; leaves alternately attached to an upright stem; often fold up during the heat of the day

Fruit: smooth flattened green pod, 1¼-2¼" (3-5.5 cm) long, turning brown; often present alongside flowers

Bloom: spring, summer, fall

Cycle/Origin: annual; native

Habitat: disturbed areas, roadsides, old fields, hammock margins and openings

Range: throughout

Notes: This showy annual is one of the most abundant and widespread legumes in Florida. Dispersed by seed, it has somewhat weedy habits and naturalizes readily. Multi-branched and shrublike, it often forms dense stands in a variety of open sunny habitats. A host plant for caterpillars of several butterflies, including Little Yellows, Cloudless Sulphurs, Gray Hairstreaks and Ceraunus Blues.

FLOWER TYPE	LEAF TYPE	LEAF ATTACHMENT	FRUIT
Irregular	**Compound**	**Alternate**	**Pod**

CAROLINA DESERT-CHICORY
Pyrrhopappus carolinianus

Family: Aster (Asteraceae)

Height: 8-24" (20-61 cm)

Flower: pale yellow flower head, 1-1½" (2.5-4 cm) wide, resembling a dandelion; composed of numerous fringe-tipped, elongated petals (ray flowers); head borne on long slender flower stalk

Leaf: elongated lance-shaped basal leaves, 7-10" (7.5-25 cm) long, form a rosette and have deep lobes or are toothed; stem leaves are much smaller and alternately attached to an upright or ascending, smooth to slightly hairy stem

Bloom: year-round

Cycle/Origin: annual, biennial; native

Habitat: roadsides, disturbed sites, fields, lawns, dry woods

Range: northern and central Florida

Notes: A common weed of dry open sites and home landscapes, this plant is often confused with Common Dandelion (pg. 365) and is even known by another common name, False Dandelion. Like a dandelion, it has a long vertical root (taproot) and contains milky sap. However, Carolina Desert-chicory is taller than that familiar weed and can be distinguished by the presence of stem leaves.

FLOWER TYPE	LEAF TYPE	LEAF TYPE	LEAF ATTACHMENT	LEAF ATTACHMENT
Composite	Simple	Simple Lobed	Alternate	Basal

FLORIDA GREEN EYES
Berlandiera subacaulis

Family: Aster (Asteraceae)

Height: 6-20" (15-50 cm)

Flower: daisy-like flower head, 1-1½" (2.5-4 cm) wide, with 8 oval, bright yellow petals (ray flowers) and a green center (disk flowers) that turns yellow when the disk flowers open; flattened green bracts below flower head; solitary head on a long, slender, upright or arching flower stalk

Leaf: oval or spatula-shaped leaves, 2-6" (5-15 cm) long, with scalloped edges; mostly basal; some upper leaves alternately attached to a slender hairy stem

Bloom: spring, summer; sometimes year-round

Cycle/Origin: perennial; native

Habitat: disturbed sites, pinelands, dry woodlands

Range: throughout, except in the western panhandle

Notes: This small but distinctive wildflower is unique (endemic) to Florida. Its common name refers to where it is found and the green "eyes" of the daisy-like yellow flower head. A common perennial with a long and thick vertical root (taproot), it thrives in a variety of dry open locations. Mature plants form sizable clumps that bear several flower stalks. While primarily a spring and summer bloomer in northern Florida counties, it may continue to flower throughout the year in southern portions of the peninsula.

FLOWER TYPE

Composite

LEAF TYPE

Simple Lobed

LEAF ATTACHMENT

Alternate

LEAF ATTACHMENT

Basal

LANCELEAF TICKSEED
Coreopsis lanceolata

Family: Aster (Asteraceae)

Height: 8-24" (20-61 cm)

Flower: solitary daisy-like flower head, 1-1½" (2.5-4 cm) wide, with several bright yellow petals (ray flowers) conspicuously notched at their tips surrounding a golden center (disk flowers); flowers atop long slender flower stalks

Leaf: lance-shaped, mostly basal leaves, 2-4½" (5-11 cm) long; the few stem leaves are opposite; leaves can sometimes have 1-2 lobes

Bloom: spring, summer

Cycle/Origin: perennial; native

Habitat: roadsides, old fields, disturbed sites

Range: northern and central Florida

Notes: One of 14 native tickseed species found in Florida and naturally distributed over most of North America. Widely grown as a garden ornamental and sold under a variety of different common names. The Florida ecotype (populations that are adapted to the environmental conditions in the state) is usually quite short and dwarfed by the common garden varieties. A hardy, drought-tolerant plant that flowers best in poor soils, it is often planted along roads.

FLOWER TYPE
Composite

LEAF TYPE
Simple

LEAF TYPE
Simple Lobed

LEAF ATTACHMENT
Opposite

LEAF ATTACHMENT
Basal

CREEPING OXEYE
Sphagneticola trilobata

Family: Aster (Asteraceae)

Height: 6-15" (15-38 cm)

Flower: large daisy-like flower head, 1-1½" (2.5-4 cm) wide, made up of several bright yellow petals (ray flowers) lobed at their tips and a gold center (disk flowers)

Leaf: elliptical or 3-lobed, shiny, dark green leaves, 1-2" (2.5-5 cm) long, with toothed edges; leaves oppositely attached to a creeping stem

Bloom: year-round

Cycle/Origin: perennial; non-native

Habitat: open woods, pinelands, coastal dunes, disturbed sites

Range: central and southern Florida

Notes: As "Creeping" in its common name suggests, this is a low-growing plant that often forms extensive mats with intertwined stems. Native to West Indies, Creeping Oxeye is regularly used as an ornamental ground cover, but has escaped cultivation and invaded many of Florida's wild lands. Because of its aggressive nature and rapid growth, this Aster family member can displace native vegetation and is considered a significant nuisance weed. Also known as Wedelia, sharing the name with *Wedelia*, the genus in which it was previously placed.

FLOWER TYPE	LEAF TYPE	LEAF TYPE	LEAF ATTACHMENT
Composite	Simple	Simple Lobed	Opposite

361

TREE SEASIDE TANSY
Borrichia arborescens

Family: Aster (Asteraceae)

Height: 1-4' (30-122 cm)

Flower: daisy-like yellow flower heads, each 1-1¾" (2.5-4.5 cm) wide, with oval, bright yellow petals (ray flowers) surrounding a large, brownish yellow center (disk flowers)

Leaf: thick, smooth, dark green leaves, 2-4" (5-10 cm) long, are lance-shaped to uniformly thin

Bloom: year-round

Cycle/Origin: perennial; native

Habitat: along salt or brackish marshes, mangrove swamps or shorelines

Range: extreme southern Florida

Notes: This evergreen woody perennial is common along Florida's coastlines, where it often forms extensive colonies. The dense and bushy plants are extremely salt tolerant and capable of thriving in the harsh conditions at the margins of salt or brackish water habitats. For these reasons, Tree Seaside Tansy is a desirable native plant addition to any coastal garden or commercial landscape. Although often overshadowed by the thick, dark green foliage, the large yellow flowers attract many butterflies and other insect pollinators.

FLOWER TYPE

Composite

LEAF TYPE

Simple

LEAF ATTACHMENT

Opposite

COMMON DANDELION
Taraxacum officinale

Family: Aster (Asteraceae)

Height: 2-18" (5-45 cm)

Flower: appears as 1 large yellow flower, 1½" (4 cm) wide, but is actually a composite of many tiny flowers that are clustered together

Leaf: rosette of basal leaves that have deep lobes and sharp teeth

Bloom: year-round

Cycle/Origin: perennial; non-native

Habitat: waste areas, disturbed sites, fields, dry soils, sun

Range: throughout

Notes: A non-native perennial that is responsible for much water contamination, as people treat lawns with chemicals to eradicate it. In French, *dent-de-lion* refers to the teeth of its leaf edge, which resemble the teeth of a lion. Its flowers open in mornings and close in afternoons. The globe-like seed heads have soft, hair-like bristles that resemble tiny parachutes, which carry the seeds away on the wind. Originally brought from Eurasia as a food crop, its leaves are bitter, but offer high vitamin and mineral content. Its long taproot can be roasted and ground to use as a coffee substitute.

FLOWER TYPE

Composite

LEAF TYPE

Simple Lobed

LEAF ATTACHMENT

Basal

PERUVIAN PRIMROSE-WILLOW
Ludwigia peruviana

Family: Evening-primrose (Onagraceae)

Height: 3-10' (.9-3 m); shrub

Flower: large showy flower, 1-2" (2.5-5 cm) wide, with 4-5 broad, bright yellow petals around a yellow center

Leaf: hairy leaves, 2-6" (5-15 cm) long, are lance-shaped to elliptical, stalkless (or nearly so) and have smooth or slightly toothed edges; alternate on a woody multi-branched stem; hairy branches when young

Fruit: cylindrical 4-angled capsule, ½-1" (1-2.5 cm) long, is upright and turns brown with age, splitting open to release seeds

Bloom: year-round

Cycle/Origin: perennial; non-native

Habitat: pond and canal margins, wet ditches, swamp edges

Range: throughout

Notes: Native to tropical America, this robust and woody shrub was introduced as an ornamental, despite the showy flowers lasting but a single day. It is now naturalized throughout much of the Southeast. Producing large amounts of seeds, Peruvian Primrose-willow spreads rapidly to colonize disturbed moist sites and wetland margins. The tall plants can grow well over 6 feet (1.8 m) wide, and often form dense stands that can clog waterways. Aggressive, it can displace native plants. The plant is of poor value to wildlife.

FLOWER TYPE	LEAF TYPE	LEAF ATTACHMENT	FRUIT
Regular	Simple	Alternate	Pod

GOLDENMANE TICKSEED
Coreopsis basalis

Family: Aster (Asteraceae)

Height: 12-30" (30-76 cm)

Flower: daisy-like flower head, 1-2" (2.5-5 cm) wide, made up of lobed, bright yellow petals (ray flowers) with reddish brown to purple at the bases that forms a band around a reddish brown center (disk flowers); blooms atop long slender flower stalks

Leaf: large basal leaves, 2½-6" (6-15 cm) long, have 3-9 lobes; thin lance-shaped stem leaves are smaller and oppositely attached to a slender upright stem

Bloom: spring, summer

Cycle/Origin: annual; native

Habitat: dry sandy soils, roadsides, fields, disturbed sites

Range: northern and central Florida

Notes: A likeness similar-looking to this species is depicted on the Florida Wildflower license plate. This lovely wildflower has become naturalized throughout much of the Southeast in sandy, open disturbed sites. Commonly planted in masses along roads and other rights-of-way, its bright flower heads provide extensive waves of yellow. Although not considered a good pollinator-attracting plant, the large blooms do attract a number of small native bees and butterflies. Also known as Dyeflower, it was used by American Indians as a source for several colors of dye.

FLOWER TYPE	LEAF TYPE	LEAF TYPE	LEAF ATTACHMENT	LEAF ATTACHMENT
Composite	Simple	Simple Lobed	Opposite	Basal

CAROLINA JESSAMINE
Gelsemium sempervirens

Family: Logania (Loganiaceae)

Height: 3-20' (.9-6.1 m); vine

Flower: large, funnel-shaped, bright yellow flower, 1-2" (2.5-5 cm) long, made of 5 petals fused on the lower half and spreading widely at the mouth; on short flower stalk; blooms in groups at leaf attachments

Leaf: shiny, lance-shaped or elliptical, dark green leaves, 1-3" (2.5-7.5 cm) long, smooth-edged and oppositely attached; slender, wiry, reddish brown stems

Fruit: flattened, pointed-tipped, elliptical green capsule, ⅝-1" (1.5-2.5 cm) long, turning reddish brown and splitting open at maturity

Bloom: winter, spring

Cycle/Origin: perennial; native

Habitat: dry to moist soils, woodlands, thickets

Range: throughout

Notes: A common woody vine of moist to dry forests, Carolina Jessamine ushers in the spring season with a prolific display of showy, fragrant, brilliant yellow flowers. It is a rapid grower and quickly rambles over shrubs and other plants of medium height, but is capable of climbing high into mature trees. Adapts easily to home landscapes and is widely popular for use on arbors or fences. *Sempervirens* means "always green," referring to the evergreen foliage. The long tubular shape of the blooms attracts hummingbirds.

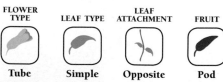

FLOWER TYPE	LEAF TYPE	LEAF ATTACHMENT	FRUIT
Tube	Simple	Opposite	Pod

BUR-MARIGOLD
Bidens laevis

Family: Aster (Asteraceae)

Height: 2-5' (61-152 cm)

Flower: showy, daisy-like, yellow flower heads; each flower, 1½-2¼" (4-5.5 cm) wide, with 8 oval yellow petals (ray flowers) surrounding a brownish yellow center (disk flowers)

Leaf: stalkless leaves, 2-6" (5-15 cm) long, with toothed edges; each leaf oppositely attached to an upright or ascending smooth stem

Bloom: summer, fall

Cycle/Origin: annual; native

Habitat: pond edges, marshes, wet ditches, lake margins

Range: throughout

Notes: Often forming extensive colonies, the showy Bur-marigold flower heads provide a display of late-season color. A true wetland specialist, it grows in a variety of low wet places, often even in standing water. "Bur" in the plant's common name refers to the two elongated, stiff bristles found on each slender seed. The burs adhere easily to clothes, feathers or animal fur and help the species spread to new locations.

FLOWER TYPE
Composite

LEAF TYPE
Simple

LEAF ATTACHMENT
Opposite

fruit

EASTERN PRICKLY PEAR
Opuntia humifusa

Family: Cactus (Cactaceae)

Height: 6-18" (15-45 cm)

Flower: large showy flower, 1½-3½" (4-9 cm) wide, of several broad overlapping yellow petals around a wide yellow center; blooms are usually solitary and grow upright from the tips of pads

Leaf: flattened fleshy pad, 2-6" (5-15 cm) long, is green and has round dark areas containing many fine bristles and often 1-2 long gray spines

Fruit: barrel-shaped green pod, 1-2" (2.5-5 cm) long, turns red to purple; often with fine hooked bristles

Bloom: spring, summer

Cycle/Origin: perennial; native

Habitat: pinelands, dry open woods, disturbed sites

Range: throughout

Notes: The most widespread and commonly encountered native cactus in Florida. Although it does grow upright, it usually sprawls along the ground and can be easily overlooked when not in flower. The bristled and often spined pads surprise unsuspecting hikers or break off to hitch a ride on shoes or pant legs. Dislodged pads will easily root from the base if placed in sandy soil. Pulp of the fruit is used to make jelly, but it can be eaten raw. The recent invasion of the non-native Cactus Moth from the Caribbean potentially threatens this and other *Opuntia* species in the southeastern United States.

FLOWER TYPE

Regular

LEAF TYPE

Spines

FRUIT

Pod

BLACK-EYED SUSAN
Rudbeckia hirta

Family: Aster (Asteraceae)

Height: 12-36" (30-91 cm)

Flower: large flower head, 2-3" (5-7.5 cm) wide; button-like brown center (disk flowers) is surrounded by 10-20 daisy-like yellow petals (ray flowers); 1 to numerous flower heads per plant

Leaf: variable-shaped, slender, very hairy leaves, 2-7" (5-18 cm) long, are toothless; each winged leafstalk clasps a hairy stem

Bloom: summer, fall

Cycle/Origin: perennial, biennial; native

Habitat: disturbed sites, roadsides, old fields, pastures, rights-of-way, forest margins, open woodlands

Range: throughout

Notes: Just who "Susan" was (referred to in the common name) remains unknown. Also called Brown-eyed Susan. One of nine species of *Rudbeckia* in Florida. The species name *hirta* is Latin for "hairy" or "rough" and refers to the plant's hairy nature. Look for the three prominent veins on each leaf and a characteristic winged leafstalk clasping each upright, straight stem. A widely utilized garden ornamental, it is now found in many habitats. It is a desirable and commonly used wildflower for large-scale naturalizing. Although this wildflower is regularly planted in butterfly gardens, the showy yellow flowers are seldom visited by butterflies.

FLOWER TYPE

Composite

LEAF TYPE

Simple

LEAF ATTACHMENT

Alternate

LEAF ATTACHMENT

Clasping

CUTLEAF CONEFLOWER
Rudbeckia laciniata

Family: Aster (Asteraceae)

Height: 5-8' (1.5-2.4 m)

Flower: each plant grows 20-50 large composite flower heads; each flower head, 2-3" (5-7.5 cm) wide, has 8-10 drooping yellow petals (ray flowers) that surround a cone-shaped green center (disk flowers)

Leaf: lower leaves, 5-8" (13-20 cm) long, have 3-5 sharp lobes and coarse teeth; upper leaves, 2-3" (5-7.5 cm) long, are simple, coarsely toothed and nearly clasp the stem

Bloom: summer, fall

Cycle/Origin: perennial; native

Habitat: wet soils, fields, ditches, disturbed sites, sun

Range: northern Florida

Notes: Cutleaf Coneflower is a common garden ornamental that forms tall, robust clumps. Look for its green center (cone) and drooping yellow petals, along with the lobed lower and simple upper leaves, to help identify. Frequently seen growing in wet ditches or along roads, it is often called Golden Glow or Green-headed Coneflower. A fantastic plant for a pollinator garden, its showy flowers provide a bounty of pollen and nectar for bees, wasps and beetles, and for butterflies such as Monarchs and fritillaries.

FLOWER TYPE	LEAF TYPE	LEAF TYPE	LEAF ATTACHMENT
Composite	Simple	Simple Lobed	Alternate

NARROWLEAF SUNFLOWER
Helianthus angustifolius

Family: Aster (Asteraceae)

Height: 4-7' (1.2-2.1 m)

Flower: daisy-like flower head, 2-3" (5-7.5 cm) wide, made up of 10-15 elongated, bright yellow petals (ray flowers) around a dark reddish brown center (disk flowers); flower heads atop long flower stalks

Leaf: long, thin, dark green basal leaves, 2-6" (5-15 cm) long, are very rough, pointed-tipped, have smooth margins and are mostly stalkless; stem leaves are shorter up the stout, upright, green-to-brown stem and alternately attached

Bloom: summer, fall

Cycle/Origin: perennial; native

Habitat: moist to dry sites, open woodlands, forest margins, old fields, roadsides

Range: northern and central Florida

Notes: One of 18 species of *Helianthus* in Florida. True to its name, Narrowleaf Sunflower can be differentiated by its thin leaves from the closely related Paleleaf Woodland Sunflower (pg. 387), which has lanced-shaped leaves. Narrowleaf's other common name, Swamp Sunflower, is somewhat of a misnomer, as Narrowleaf can be found in drier upland sites as well as moist habitats. This robust, late-season wildflower produces a spectacular display of large yellow blooms. The seeds are eaten by songbirds and small mammals.

FLOWER TYPE	LEAF TYPE	LEAF ATTACHMENT	LEAF ATTACHMENT

Composite	**Simple**	**Alternate**	**Basal**

PALELEAF WOODLAND SUNFLOWER
Helianthus strumosus

Family: Aster (Asteraceae)

Height: 2-6' (.6-1.8 m)

Flower: daisy-like flower head, 2½-3¼" (6-8 cm) wide, composed of long, oval, bright yellow petals (ray flowers) around a golden center (disk flowers); flower head sits atop a long flower stalk

Leaf: rough lance-shaped leaves, 4-6½" (10-16 cm) long, are dark green above, pale to whitish green below, and have rounded bases, pointed tips and narrowly toothed edges; oppositely attached with short leaf-stalks to a stout, upright, green-to-brown stem

Bloom: summer, fall

Cycle/Origin: perennial; native

Habitat: open woodlands, forest edges, along roads

Range: northern Florida

Notes: The large yellow flowers of Paleleaf Woodland Sunflower brighten up partially shaded confines of forest margins and areas dappled with sunlight under tree canopies. Aggressively spreads by underground stems (rhizomes) to form extensive, dense colonies and should not be planted in small landscapes. Hybridizes with the closely related Woodland Sunflower (*H. divaricatus*) (not shown), making it challenging, if not impossible, to tell them apart in the wild. The showy blooms provide ample resources for pollinating insects. Its seeds are a favorite late-season food of many songbirds.

FLOWER TYPE	LEAF TYPE	LEAF ATTACHMENT
Composite	**Simple**	**Opposite**

fruit

AMERICAN LOTUS
Nelumbo lutea

Family: Lotus (Nelumbonaceae)

Height: aquatic

Flower: cup-shaped, pale yellow flower, 6-10" (15-25 cm) wide; many large petals surround a large yellow center; flowers stand up to 12" (30 cm) above the water's surface

Leaf: very large, round leaves, 12-24" (30-61 cm) wide, are toothless and stand up to 12" (30 cm) above the surface of the water; edges are often upturned to form a shallow bowl

Fruit: round pod-like green container, turning brown; numerous acorn-like seeds are released through many Swiss cheese-like openings at the top

Bloom: summer, fall

Cycle/Origin: perennial; native

Habitat: small lakes, ponds, slow-moving waterways

Range: throughout

Notes: This plant's large round leaves and large flowers stand well above the water, waving in the wind, distinguishing the plant from water-lilies. Its flowers open only on sunny days, giving rise to the large seedpods often used in dried floral arrangements. Like water-lilies, its roots are eaten by wildlife, and its seeds and roots were used as food by American Indians. The seeds were also used as counters and dice in games. One of two lotus species found in Florida.

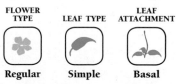

FLOWER TYPE	LEAF TYPE	LEAF ATTACHMENT	FRUIT
Regular	Simple	Basal	Pod

DOLLARLEAF
Rhynchosia reniformis

Family: Pea or Bean (Fabaceae)

Height: 2-8" (5-20 cm)

Flower: small spike cluster, ½-1" (1-2.5 cm) long, densely packed with several pea-like, bright yellow flowers; each flower, ¼" (.6 cm) long, with 5 petals

Leaf: appears like a single, round or kidney-shaped leaf, ¾-2½" (2-6 cm) wide, but is actually a compound leaf that is unifoliate (having only 1 leaflet, rarely 2-3); alternately attached to a stout hairy stem

Fruit: small, hairy and flattened, bean-like green pod, ½-¾" (1-2 cm) long, turning brown at maturity and splitting open to release seeds

Bloom: spring, summer, fall

Cycle/Origin: perennial; native

Habitat: dry open woodlands, pinelands, sandhills, forest margins, sandy roadsides

Range: northern two-thirds of Florida

Notes: The species name *reniformis* is for the plant's distinctive, kidney-shaped leaves. "Dollar" in the common name refers to the overall leaf size, which is similar to that of a silver dollar coin. Keeping these leaf shape and size characteristics in mind can help when attempting to identify this short upright plant in the wild. Occurs in small colonies and is often is particularly abundant in areas following natural or prescribed fires.

CLUSTER TYPE	FLOWER TYPE	LEAF TYPE	LEAF ATTACHMENT	FRUIT
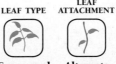				
Spike	Irregular	Compound	Alternate	Pod

NARROWLEAF YELLOWTOPS
Flaveria linearis

Family: Aster (Asteraceae)

Height: 12-36" (30-91 cm)

Flower: large dense flat cluster, 1-4" (2.5-10 cm) wide, composed of many small golden flower heads; each flower head made up of tubular disk flowers and usually lacks petals (ray flowers), but sometimes will have a single petal

Leaf: uniformly thin or narrowly lance-shaped green leaves, 2-4" (5-10 cm) long, opposite on any branched stem; new stems are often reddish green

Bloom: year-round

Cycle/Origin: perennial; native

Habitat: coastal areas, hammock margins, pinelands

Range: central and southern Florida

Notes: Of the four yellowtops species in Florida, Narrowleaf Yellowtops is by far the most widespread and common. The densely branched plants form spreading mounds that tend to be much broader than tall. Both "Narrowleaf" in the common name and the species name *linearis* refer to the profuse, uniformly thin leaves that adorn the stems. The prominent golden flower clusters are a favorite of many butterflies and other insects. Easily grown and highly ornamental, Narrowleaf Yellowtops is a drought- and pest-resistant plant that makes an ideal addition to any garden.

CLUSTER TYPE	FLOWER TYPE	LEAF TYPE	LEAF ATTACHMENT
Flat	Composite	Simple	Opposite

CHAPMAN GOLDENROD
Solidago odora chapmanii

Family: Aster (Asteraceae)

Height: 3-5' (.9-1.5 m)

Flower: spike clusters, 1½-4" (4-10 cm) long, of numerous small, tubular, upright, yellow flower heads; flower heads are borne along 1 side of and on the upper portions of flower stalks

Leaf: lance-shaped leaves, 1½-4" (4-10 cm) long, are stalkless and alternate on a slender, upright, often arching stem

Bloom: summer, fall

Cycle/Origin: perennial; native

Habitat: dry or sandy sites, woodlands, pinelands, roadsides, waste areas

Range: throughout Florida, except in the panhandle

Notes: A common wildflower of dry woodlands, it tends to be somewhat less conspicuous or showy than many other species of goldenrod. One of two varieties of this species occurring in Florida. The other, var. *odora* (not shown) and called Sweet Goldenrod due to its mild, anise-scented foliage, occurs mostly in the panhandle portion of the state. Chapman Goldenrod is nearly identical to Sweet, but Chapman lacks the aromatic leaves.

CLUSTER TYPE	FLOWER TYPE	LEAF TYPE	LEAF ATTACHMENT
Spike	Tube	Simple	Alternate

in seed

CANADA GOLDENROD
Solidago canadensis

Family: Aster (Asteraceae)

Height: 2-5' (61-152 cm)

Flower: mass of individual yellow flower heads, ¼" (.6 cm) wide, arranged in large arching spike clusters, 3-9" (7.5-23 cm) long; tip of the tallest flower cluster nods to 1 side

Leaf: narrow leaves, up to 6" (15 cm) long, are rough to the touch and have smooth margins; fewer leaves near the base of stem

Bloom: summer, fall

Cycle/Origin: perennial; native

Habitat: open disturbed sites, old fields, roadsides, open forests, along fencerows

Range: northern and central Florida

Notes: This common plant, often seen in roadside patches, reproduces by sending up new plants from roots (clones), creating patches as wide as 8-30 feet (2.4-9.1 m), excluding other plants from the site. Over 100 types of goldenrod in North America, with over 20 in Florida. All look similar, thus are hard to identify. While most yellow autumn flowers are a type of goldenrod and are often blamed for hay fever, most hay fever is caused by ragweed. Only 1-2 percent of autumn airborne pollen is from goldenrod. Goldenrod is pollinated by insects, such as flies, beetles, ambush bugs, midges and bees, that are attracted to the flower's abundant nectar.

CLUSTER TYPE	FLOWER TYPE	LEAF TYPE	LEAF ATTACHMENT
Spike	Composite	Simple	Alternate

SLENDER FLAT-TOPPED GOLDENROD
Euthamia caroliniana

Family: Aster (Asteraceae)

Height: 10-36" (25-91 cm)

Flower: ragged flat cluster, 2-11" (5-28 cm) wide, made up of numerous tiny, golden yellow flower heads, each less than ⅛" (.4 cm) long

Leaf: numerous uniformly thin leaves, ¾-2¾" (2-7 cm) long, alternately attached to a slender upright stem that becomes branched at the upper end

Bloom: summer, fall

Cycle/Origin: perennial; native

Habitat: disturbed sites, roadsides, old fields, forest edges, pinelands

Range: throughout

Notes: This showy, yellow-flowered plant is not a true goldenrod, despite the latter part of its common name and its similar overall appearance to those plants. However, it is closely related and was even previously placed in the genus *Solidago*, of which goldenrods are members. Usually occurring in small but dense colonies, Slender Flat-topped Goldenrods prefer dry sites in sunny or partially shaded habitats. The upright, airy clusters burst into full bloom in late summer and in autumn, becoming an important nectar source for bees and butterflies.

CLUSTER TYPE	FLOWER TYPE	LEAF TYPE	LEAF ATTACHMENT
Flat	Composite	Simple	Alternate

fruit

SHOWY RATTLEBOX
Crotalaria spectabilis

Family: Pea or Bean (Fabaceae)

Height: 3-8' (.9-2.4 m)

Flower: spike cluster, 4-12" (10-30 cm) long, of large, bright yellow flowers, ⅔-1" (1.6-2.5 cm) long; flowers have 5 petals and bloom from the base of spike upward

Leaf: paddle-shaped leaves, 2-6" (5-15 cm) long, smooth above and hairy beneath; alternately attached to a smooth, often branched stem

Fruit: smooth inflated cylindrical pod, 1-2" (2.5-5 cm) long, with thin pointed tip; pod is initially pale green, turning black at maturity; splits open to release bean-like seeds

Bloom: summer, fall

Cycle/Origin: annual; non-native

Habitat: disturbed areas, roadsides, old fields, pastures

Range: throughout

Notes: A robust, showy-flowered legume of open disturbed sites. Originally introduced from Indo-Malaysia as a soil-building cover crop for sandy soils, it escaped into the wild and is now naturalized throughout the Southeast, where it is a weed of agricultural landscapes and pastures. Spread by seed, it often occurs in large stands. All parts (especially the seeds) of the plant are toxic to livestock and humans. Mature seeds often break loose inside the large and inflated, bean-like pods and make a rattling sound when shaken.

CLUSTER TYPE	FLOWER TYPE	LEAF TYPE	LEAF ATTACHMENT	FRUIT
		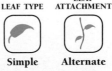		
Spike	Irregular	Simple	Alternate	Pod

fruit

YELLOW NICKER
Caesalpinia bonduc

Family: Pea or Bean (Fabaceae)

Height: 4-15' (1.2-4.6 m); shrub

Flower: large dense spike cluster, 6-10" (15-25 cm) long, of many fragrant, small, brownish yellow flowers; each flower ⅓" (.8 cm) wide, with 5 widely flaring petals

Leaf: compound leaves, 10-18" (25-45 cm) long, are dark green, shiny, stalked and have paired elliptical leaflets, each ¾-1½" (2-4 cm) long; underside bases of leaflets have short curved spines; thick sprawling woody stem has many sharp straight thorns

Fruit: large, oblong, spiny green pod, 2-3" (5-7.5 cm) long, turning brown and splitting open to reveal 1-3 round hard gray seeds

Bloom: summer, fall

Cycle/Origin: perennial; native

Habitat: coastal dunes, shorelines, forest openings

Range: central and southern Florida

Notes: A robust, fast-growing, vine-like shrub of coastal habitats. Scrambles over open ground or low vegetation, but can climb into the canopies of small trees. An unassuming beachgoer may get bloodied while trying to navigate through the extensive, nearly impenetrable thickets formed by the thorn-laden branches. Its spiny, clam-shaped pods are a tourist curiosity. The seeds are well adapted for traveling between islands or long distances on ocean currents.

CLUSTER TYPE	FLOWER TYPE	LEAF TYPE	LEAF ATTACHMENT	FRUIT
Spike	Irregular	Compound	Alternate	Pod

fruit

BANDANNA-OF-THE-EVERGLADES
Canna flaccida

Family: Canna (Cannaceae)

Height: 1-4' (30-122 cm)

Flower: spike cluster, 6-12" (15-30 cm) long, of a few pure yellow flowers, 2½-3" (6-7.5 cm) wide, each appearing irregular, with what looks like large upright petals, but what are actually modified flower parts (stamens and style); the true petals are bent backward from the base of the flower

Leaf: large broad shiny leaves, 18-30" (45-76 cm) long, are thick with smooth margins, and taper to a point at the tips and bases; attached to an upright stem

Fruit: elliptical green capsule, 1½-2" (4-5 cm) long, turning brown and releasing several round brown seeds

Bloom: year-round

Cycle/Origin: perennial; native

Habitat: moist soils, pond margins, marshes

Range: throughout

Notes: Found in a variety of seasonally wet habitats, Bandanna-of-the-Everglades spreads by rhizomes and can establish large colonies. Also called Golden Canna, the showy, pure yellow flowers above the thick green leaves provide a spectacular display when in masses. Often planted in garden landscapes. A host plant for the long, semi-transparent caterpillars of Brazilian Skippers, which fold over the leaf edges and seal them with silk, creating individual shelters.

CLUSTER TYPE	FLOWER TYPE	LEAF TYPE	LEAF ATTACHMENT	LEAF ATTACHMENT	FRUIT
Spike	Tube	Simple	Alternate	Clasping	Pod

YELLOW NECKLACEPOD
Sophora tomentosa

Family: Pea or Bean (Fabaceae)

Height: 3-10' (.9-3 m); shrub

Flower: dense spike cluster, 5-16" (13-40 cm) long, of many pea-like, bright yellow flowers; each flower, ½-¾" (.1-2 cm) long

Leaf: evergreen compound leaves, 8-12" (20-30 cm) long, made up of numerous paired glossy oval leaflets; each leaflet, ¾-2" (2-5 cm) long; leaves on long stalks and alternate on multi-branched woody stem

Fruit: long, drooping, pale yellow pod, 3-8" (7.5-20 cm) long, is very compressed between the seeds; turns brown with age; pods and flowers may be present on the plant at the same time

Bloom: year-round

Cycle/Origin: perennial; native

Habitat: coastal areas, hammocks

Range: southern Florida

Notes: A rounded and woody large shrub, its bright flowers attract many species of butterflies (Mangrove Skippers in particular). The pale yellow seedpods are constricted between the seeds and look like pearl necklaces, thus the common name. Easy to grow and highly ornamental. Two varieties occur in Florida. One variety, *occidentalis*, is non-native, more readily available for purchase than the *truncata* variety and can be distinguished by its velvety, silvery green foliage.

CLUSTER TYPE	FLOWER TYPE	LEAF TYPE	LEAF ATTACHMENT	FRUIT
Spike	Irregular	Compound	Alternate	Pod

fruit

LANCELEAF RATTLEBOX
Crotalaria lanceolata

Family: Pea or Bean (Fabaceae)

Height: 18-36" (45-91 cm)

Flower: long narrow spike cluster, 10-18" (25-45 cm) long, of many small, pea-like, yellow flowers marked with red lines; each flower, ⅜" (.9 cm) long, has 5 petals; flower spikes upright or arching

Leaf: compound leaves, of 3 uniformly narrow to lance-shaped leaflets; each leaflet, 2-4" (5-10 cm) long; leaves alternate on an upright branched stem

Fruit: smooth inflated cylindrical pod, ¾-1½" (2-4 cm) long, with a thin pointed tip; pod initially green, turning brown to black at maturity and splitting open to release bean-like seeds

Bloom: year-round

Cycle/Origin: annual; non-native

Habitat: disturbed sites, open woods, fields

Range: throughout

Notes: This native of Africa is a tropical weed that has naturalized throughout Florida. Although not nearly as spectacular as the related and more statuesque Showy Rattlebox (pg. 405), Lanceleaf Rattlebox is equally abundant in open disturbed landscapes as Showy. Lanceleaf is the host for caterpillars of Bella Moth, a beautifully colored, day-flying member of the order Lepidoptera, which includes moths and butterflies.

CLUSTER TYPE	FLOWER TYPE	LEAF TYPE	LEAF ATTACHMENT	FRUIT
Spike	Irregular	Simple	Alternate	Pod

SEASIDE GOLDENROD
Solidago sempervirens

Family: Aster (Asteraceae)

Height: 2-6' (.6-1.8 m)

Flower: tightly packed, cylindrical spike cluster, 10-24" (25-61 cm) long, of numerous small yellow flower heads; each flower head composed of 7-10 petals (ray flowers) around a yellow center (disk flowers); spikes are at the end of flower stalks

Leaf: fleshy, smooth, elliptical basal leaves, 6-12" (15-30 cm) long; stem leaves are numerous, alternate, stalkless and much smaller going up toward the flower cluster

Bloom: summer, fall

Cycle/Origin: perennial; native

Habitat: wet pinelands, roadside ditches, coastal marshes, dune margins

Range: throughout

Notes: As "Seaside" in the common name implies, this distinctive wildflower is found in a variety of coastal habitats. Attractive and salt tolerant, Seaside Goldenrod is an excellent addition to Florida gardens. It is readily available for purchase from many garden centers with native plants. The showy flower cluster is long and cylindrical, resembling a king's scepter, and attracts a variety of pollinating insects. Spreading by both seed and underground stems (rhizomes), it often forms large clumps of plants over time.

CLUSTER TYPE	FLOWER TYPE	LEAF TYPE	LEAF ATTACHMENT	LEAF ATTACHMENT
Spike	Composite	Simple	Alternate	Basal

WAND MULLEIN
Verbascum virgatum

Family: Snapdragon (Scrophulariaceae)

Height: 3-6' (.9-1.8 m)

Flower: wand-like spike cluster, 12-32" (30-80 cm) long, with stalked flowers; each flower, 1-1½" (2.5-4 cm) long, composed of 5 broad yellow petals with a purple center

Leaf: elliptical leaves, 3-12" (7.5-30 cm) long, with toothed edges; basal leaves are larger and stalked; stem leaves alternate and clasping; leaves get progressively smaller going up along the stalk

Bloom: summer, fall, winter

Cycle/Origin: biennial; non-native

Habitat: roadsides, old fields, disturbed sites

Range: northern and central Florida

Notes: This native European wildflower was introduced into the U.S. and has since naturalized in many states. Wand Mullein can thrive in a variety of habitats and spreads rapidly by producing a large amount of seeds. Considered a "pioneer plant," one of the first species to colonize in disturbed areas along roads or in pastures or old fields. The first year it grows as a low rosette of basal leaves; a tall flower stalk sprouts in the second. In fact, the species name *virgatum* means "twiggy" or "wand-like," referring to the stalk.

CLUSTER TYPE	FLOWER TYPE	LEAF TYPE	LEAF ATTACHMENT	LEAF ATTACHMENT	LEAF ATTACHMENT
Spike	Regular	Simple	Alternate	Clasping	Basal

417

GLOSSARY

Alternate: A type of leaf attachment in which the leaves are singly and alternately attached along a stem, not paired or in whorls.

Annual: A plant that germinates, flowers and sets seed during a single growing season and returns the following year from seed only.

Anther: A portion of the male flower part that contains the pollen. See *stamen*.

Axis: A point on the main stem from which lateral branches arise.

Basal: The leaves at the base of a plant near the ground, usually grouped in a round rosette.

Bell flower: A single, downward-hanging flower that has petals fused together, forming a bell-like shape. See *tube flower*.

Berry: A fleshy fruit that contains one or many seeds.

Biennial: A plant that lives for two years, blooming in the second year.

Bract: A leaf-like structure usually found at the base of a flower, often appearing as a petal.

Bulb: A short, round, underground shoot that is used as a food storage system, common in the Lily family.

Calyx: A collective group of all of the sepals of a flower.

Capsule: A pod-like fruiting structure that contains many seeds and has more than one chamber. See *pod*.

Cauline: The leaves that attach to the stem distinctly above the ground, as opposed to basal leaves, which attach near the ground.

Clasping: A type of leaf attachment in which the leaf base partly surrounds the main stem of the plant at the point of attachment; grasping the stem without a leafstalk.

Cluster: A group or collection of flowers or leaves.

Composite flower: A collection of tiny or small flowers that appears as one large flower, usually made up of ray and disk flowers, common in the Aster family.

Compound leaf: A single leaf composed of a central stalk and two or more leaflets.

Corolla: All of the petals of a flower that fuse together to form a tube.

Disk flower: One of many tiny, tubular flowers in the central part (disk) of a composite flower, common in the Aster family.

Endemic: Unique or exclusive to a particular geographic region or area.

Ephemeral: Lasting for only a short time each spring.

Flat cluster: A group of flowers that forms a flat-topped structure, which allows flying insects to easily land and complete pollination.

Gland: A tiny structure that usually secretes oil or nectar, sometimes found on leaves, stems, stalks and flowers, as in Partridge Pea.

Hammock: A forested small hill or knoll next to a marshy area in the southern United States; also known as a hummock.

Irregular flower: A flower that does not have the typical round shape, usually made up of five or more petals that are fused together in an irregular shape, common in the Pea or Bean family.

Keel: The two lower petals, often fused together, of a flower in the Pea or Bean family.

Leaflet: One of two or more leaf-like parts of a compound leaf.

Lip: The projection of a flower petal or the "odd" petal, such as the large inflated petal common in the Snapdragon family; sometimes, the lobes of a petal. See *lobe*.

Lobe: A large rounded projection of a petal or leaf, larger than the tooth of a leaf.

Lobed leaf: A simple leaf with at least one indentation (sinus) along an edge that does not reach the center or base of the leaf, as in Common Dandelion.

Margin: The edge of a leaf.

Node: The place or point of origin on a stem where leaves attach or have been attached.

Nutlet: A small or diminutive nut or seed.

Opposite: A type of leaf attachment in which pairs of leaves are situated directly across from each other on a stem.

Palmate leaf: A type of compound leaf in which three or more leaflets arise from a common central point at the end of a leafstalk, as in Wild Lupine.

Perennial: A plant that lives from several to many seasons, returning each year from its roots.

Perfoliate: A type of leaf attachment in which the bases of at least two leaves connect around the main stem so that the stem appears to pass through one stalkless leaf.

Petal: A basic flower part that is usually brightly colored, serving to attract pollinating insects.

Photosynthesis: In green plants, the conversion of water and carbon dioxide into carbohydrates (food) from the energy in sunlight.

Pistil: The female part of a flower made up of an ovary, style and stigma, often in the center of the flower.

Pod: A dry fruiting structure that contains many seeds, often with a single chamber. See *capsule*.

Pollination: The transfer of pollen from the male anther to the female stigma, usually resulting in the production of seeds.

Ray flower: One of many individual outer flowers of a composite flower, common in the Aster family.

Regular flower: A flower with 3-20 typical petals that are arranged in a circle.

Rhizome: A creeping, (usually) horizontal, underground stem.

Rosette: A cluster of leaves arranged in a circle, often at the base of the plant, as in Wand Mullein.

Round cluster: A group of many flowers that forms a round structure, giving the appearance of one large flower.

Seed head: A group or cluster of seeds

Semiparasitic: A type of plant that derives a portion, but not all, of its food or water from another plant, possibly to the detriment of the host plant.

Sepal: A member of the outermost set of petals of a flower, typically green and leaf-like, but often colored and resembling a petal.

Simple leaf: A single leaf with an undivided or unlobed edge.

Spike cluster: A group of many flowers on a single, spike-like stem, giving the appearance of one large flower.

Spine: A modified leaf; a stiff, usually short, sharply pointed outgrowth. See *thorn*.

Spur: A hollow, tube-like appendage of a flower, usually where nectar is located, as in Canada Toadflax.

Stamen: The male parts of a flower, each consisting of a filament and an anther. See *anther*.

Standard: The uppermost petal of a flower in the Pea or Bean family.

Stem leaf: Any leaf that grows along the stem of a plant, as opposed to a leaf at the base of a plant. See *cauline* and *basal*.

Stigma: The female part of the flower that receives the pollen.

Taproot: The primary, vertically descending root of a plant.

Tendril: A twining, string-like structure of a vine that clings to plants or other objects for support.

Terminal: Growing at the end of a leaf, stem or stalk.

Thorn: A modified part of a stem; a stiff, usually long and sharply pointed outgrowth. See *spine*.

Throat: The opening or orifice of a tubular flower (corolla or calyx).

Toothed: Having a jagged or serrated edge of a leaf, resembling teeth of a saw.

Tube flower: A flower with fused petals forming a tube and usually turned upward. See *bell flower*.

Umbel: A domed to relatively flat-topped flower cluster that resembles the overall shape of an open umbrella, common in the Carrot family.

Whorl: A type of attachment in which a circle or ring of three or more similar leaves, stems or flowers originate from a common point.

Wing: A flat extension at the base of a leaf or edge of a leafstalk, sometimes extending down the stem of the plant; one of the side petals of a flower, common in the Pea or Bean family.

Woody: Having the appearance or texture resembling wood, as in stems, bark or taproots.

CHECKLIST/INDEX

Use the boxes to check wildflowers you've seen.

422

ABOUT THE AUTHORS

Jaret C. Daniels

Jaret C. Daniels, Ph.D., is a professional nature photographer, author, native plant enthusiast and entomologist at the University of Florida, specializing in insect ecology and conservation. He has authored numerous scientific papers, popular articles and books on gardening, wildlife conservation, insects and butterflies, including *Butterflies of Florida Field Guide*, as well as butterfly field guides for Georgia, the Carolinas, Ohio and Michigan. He currently lives in Gainesville, Florida, with his wife, Stephanie.

Stan Tekiela

Naturalist, wildlife photographer and writer Stan Tekiela is the originator of the popular state-specific field guide series that includes *Birds of Florida Field Guide*. Stan has authored more than 190 educational books, including field guides, quick guides, nature books, children's books, playing cards and more, presenting many species of animals and plants.

With a Bachelor of Science degree in Natural History from the University of Minnesota and as an active professional naturalist for more than 30 years, Stan studies and photographs wildlife throughout the United States and Canada. He has received various national and regional awards for his books and photographs. Also a well-known columnist and radio personality, his syndicated column appears in more than 25 newspapers, and his wildlife programs are broadcast on a number of Midwest radio stations. Stan can be followed on Facebook and Twitter. He can be contacted via www.naturesmart.com.